WAR WITHOUT END

WAR WITHOUT END

The View from Abroad

BRUNO TERTRAIS

Translated by Franklin Philip

THE NEW PRESS

NEW YORK
LONDON

Requests for permission to reproduce selections from this book should be
mailed to: Permissions Department, The New Press, 38 Greene Street,
New York, NY 10013

Published in the United States by The New Press, New York, 2005
Originally published in France as *La Guerre sans fin: L'Amérique dans l'engrenage*
by Editions du Seuil, Paris, 2004
Distributed by W. W. Norton & Company, Inc., New York

Published with the generous support of the Florence Gould Foundation.

LIBRARY OF CONGRESS CATALOGING-IN-PUBLICATION DATA
Tertrais, Bruno.
[Guerre sans fin. English]
War without end : the view from abroad / Bruno Tertrais ; translated by
Franklin Philip.
p. cm.
Includes bibliographical references.
ISBN 1-56584-963-9
1. United States—Foreign relations—2001– 2. War on Terrorism, 2001–
I. Philip, Franklin. II. Title.

E895.T47 2005
327.73'009'0511—dc22
2004060989

The New Press was established in 1990 as a not-for-profit alternative to the large,
commercial publishing houses currently dominating the book publishing industry.
The New Press operates in the public interest rather than for private gain, and is
committed to publishing, in innovative ways, works of educational, cultural,
and community value that are often deemed insufficiently profitable.

www.thenewpress.com

Composition by Westchester Book Composition

Printed in the United States of America

2 4 6 8 10 9 7 5 3 1

For my father

CONTENTS

We are at a critical moment in history—at what promises to be the opening skirmishes of the Fourth World War. Indeed, we have embarked on what may perhaps be the most deadly war of any fought in recorded time—a war that, even more than the promise of nuclear holocaust held out by the Third World War, the cold war, has the very real prospect of ending civilization, at least Western civilization, as we know it.

What will it take to strike terror into the hearts of those who would use the physical and intellectual weapons of terrorism without fear of retaliation because of a collective failure of will on the part of their enemies? Indeed, what happens in the Fourth World War if terrorists or their national champions make use of atomic, biological, or chemical weapons that will make any conflict that has gone before barely a shadow of war?

The Fourth World War will be a terrorist war. There will be certain nations of the South that will use terrorism more effectively, more predictably as an instrument of war and military or state policy than other nations. Today, it is clear that Libya, Syria, Iran, and Iraq, for instance, are the principal supporters of this kind of warfare. Moreover, there are certain traditions in each, deep forces within their history, that make them more likely than others to turn to terrorism as a weapon of battle against the North.

The fact is that neither major power has ever truly been organized to fight the Fourth World War as we are coming to know it—but the Americans, in my opinion, are the least prepared of all. . . . My hope for the future enlightenment of the Americans springs from . . . the certainty that international terrorism will finally find its way to their shores. That is not something I would wish on my most mortal enemy, let alone my friends. But if the terrorist threat has the effect of shaking up the American people, and especially their leadership, then perhaps it will be of some value. The Americans, until now, have led a relatively charmed and sheltered existence.

—Alexandre de Marenches and David A. Andelman,
*The Fourth World War: Diplomacy and Espionage
in the Age of Terrorism* (1992)

FOREWORD TO THE U.S. EDITION

THIS IS AN expanded and updated version of a book published in France in early 2004. Since this work was originally intended for a primarily French audience, I was both surprised and flattered when André Schiffrin of The New Press approached me and convinced me that it would also be of interest to a North American and a broader English-speaking audience. Come to think of it, though, since a number of good works on French history and policies have been written by American authors, perhaps a French analysis of U.S. strategy and the war on terror could be of interest on the other side of the Atlantic.

I wrote this book to fill what I perceived to be an intellectual void. Most French men and women were opposed to the war in Iraq. A few politicians, authors, and artists took the opposite position, and heavily criticized the alleged anti-U.S. (more often anti-Bush) bias of the majority of the French population and media. But polarization is not always a sign of healthy intellectual debate—and in any case I personally felt uncomfortable with it. This is true in particular because the description of U.S. policies on both sides of the Atlantic is too often presented in a single color—generally black, sometimes white. The job of those of us in the academic world is often to unsimplify things, and there are many things to unsimplify in the debate about the war on terror, as well as a few conspiracy theories to debunk.

Like most of my countrymen, I greatly admire U.S. society without necessarily agreeing with U.S. policies. Nevertheless, I happened to support many of the goals of the Bush administration. I also felt that the administration's policies were often unjustly demonized by many analysts on both sides of the Atlantic. That put me very much at ease to criticize the way the war on terrorism and its ramifications were unfolding. On Iraq, for instance, I thought that the war was both legitimate *and* dangerous. I believed there were perfectly good strategic, political, and legal (yes, legal) reasons to go to war. However, I also thought that nothing could justify risking the lives of hundreds of thousands of Western soldiers at this particular point in time, when UN inspectors were still trying to sort out the mystery of Saddam Hussein's weapons of mass destruction programs—then the primary stated rationale for toppling the regime. I did *not* believe that stability in the Middle East was something to be preserved at all costs. Excessive stability has proven deadly, an essential factor in the development of fanatical terrorism. But I *did* believe—and I still do—that taking historical gambles requires enormous care when failure or backlash promises to be catastrophic.

While no author can claim to be immune to intellectual biases, I therefore tried to write this book in a dispassionate way, neither with an anti-U.S. nor a pro-U.S. stance. I was fortunate enough in my career, both in government and outside government, to have had access to influential figures on the U.S. scene as well as many officials in successive administrations. Some of them were to become (and still are) my friends. I certainly cannot claim to be as familiar with the Washington scene as many American authors are. But I have benefited from hindsights that certainly most Europeans, and probably most Americans, do not have. This gives me an ability to have what I believe is a fairly good understanding of U.S. policy from the outside. Writing this book was an opportunity to share my views with a broad audience in France, and I'm delighted now to share them with U.S. and other English-speaking readers.

Since I finished the manuscript of the original French text in December 2003, many events have occurred on the international scene, but none to infirm my thesis. The optimistic hubris of preventive military action is now dampened. But the war will continue for a long time, and the threats the post–September 11 U.S. strategy was meant to reduce have far from disappeared and have even grown to some extent. We're in for what may be termed one day the Long War, to reverse the expression used by John Lewis Gaddis about the East-West confrontation. As a citizen, I regret it. As an author, intellectual honesty requires that I feel vindicated. In any case, it made the additional research and writing required for this new edition an intellectual pleasure much more than a commercial duty.

I make no apologies for being a pessimist, but I would welcome arguments and events that contradict and even negate the core thesis of this book. If, on the contrary, I'm proven right, it is my wish that my readers will at least find, in their personal or spiritual life, reasons to hope.

This conflict was begun on the timing and terms of others. It will end at a time and in a way of our choosing.

—George W. Bush, September 14, 2001[1]

...it may never end. At least, not in our lifetime.

—Richard B. Cheney, October 19, 2001[2]

INTRODUCTION: BACK TO HISTORY

THE WAR HAS only begun.

In 1992, Alexandre de Marenches, a former head of the French secret services, had announced that a "fourth world war" was brewing; it would be a war against terrorism, a war that would call into question the very existence of Western civilization and for which the United States was particularly ill-prepared.[3]

In 1997 Ralph Peters, a U.S. officer in charge of future studies in the army staff, had warned, "There will be no peace." The United States of President Bill Clinton lived under the illusion of a democratization of the world through international trade and the spread of information technologies. For America, the great problems of international security were no longer of an ideological and political nature, but were about the environment, public health, poverty, and organized crime. Military force was used only reluctantly and sparingly. Engaged in promoting democracy and liberalism through business and political dialogue, the United States was blind to the accumulation of resentment in the face of the unequaled power and influence of the leading world power. It didn't understand that U.S. superiority carried war within it, for it attracted "hatred, jealousy, and greed."[4]

The United States was "on a holiday from history."[5] But history was not over. In his criticism of Francis Fukuyama, Pierre Hassner had warned that the great developed nations that had escaped from history would not be peaceful for all that, for they could be affected by the painful transition at work in the rest of the world.[6]

The Islamists affiliated with the Al Qaeda movement had already targeted U.S. interests: in Yemen in 1992, in New York in 1993, in Somalia in 1995, and in Saudi Arabia in 1996. And the United States had been the target of attacks beginning in 1983.[7] In thirty years the terrorism of Arab and Islamist origin had produced some one thousand deaths in total.[8] The war had thus already begun—but on one side only, even if, in the view of the terrorists, it was only revenge for decades of U.S. policy in the Middle East.[9] On September 11, 2001, everything changed. Just a few minutes after the attacks in New York and Washington, George W. Bush would conclude, "We are at war."[10] In one morning a small group of terrorists had put an end to "a decade in which America drifted lazily along on waters untroubled by the riptides of history."[11]

Since then the world has not stopped wondering about the motives and objectives of this war. Rarely has the United States had such a negative image as it has under Mr. Bush. Its president is seen as a trigger-happy cowboy, all the more dangerous because he is allegedly driven by profound religious convictions. Analysts frequently attribute murky motives to the White House, from the conquest of oil resources to the establishment of a new empire.

True, the times are exceptional. As Great Britain mastered the seas, the United States "[has] command [of] the commons," to use an expression forged by analyst Barry Posen, that is, the maritime, air, spatial, and electronic media.[12] But never had the world known the union of military superiority, ideological vision, and political unilateralism in the absence of any serious competitor. In the nineteenth century, England came up against Russia. In the late twentieth century the United States had no plan for remodeling the world. In this context, one can understand why the hypothesis of an outburst of imperial power is so popular.

But the U.S. strategy calls for a more rigorous analysis. Both simpler and more complex than it seems, this strategy probably doesn't warrant the excessive honors done to it by its admirers, but even less the shamefulness that frequently characterizes the commentaries about it in Europe and elsewhere. The analyses done in the United States in support of the country's foreign policy are often deeper and subtler than many believe. Conversely, U.S. motives are not as cynical, not as complex as is claimed, and it will be useful to put an end to certain preconceived ideas.

But though the criticisms of it are often excessive, the U.S. strategy nevertheless reveals ideological and religious dimensions that make it sometimes even more troubling than its caricature. For the attacks of September 11 have served as a catalyst for the expression of political forces whose agenda goes well beyond the mere protection of the national territory and that have transformed what could have remained a simple reduction of the threat into a combat of historical dimensions.

More than three years after September 11, everything contributes to making the logic of war prevail for a long time over the forces of moderation. The neoconservative plan got bogged down in the sands of Mesopotamia, but the dynamics of the "global war against terrorism" remain. The U.S. political culture was profoundly transformed by September 11: there will be no going back in time. Moreover, the White House and the Pentagon no longer control the scenario. On both sides, extremist forces fuel the tensions. Islamic and Protestant fundamentalisms are becoming stronger, terrorism and proliferation are growing. Finally, the very nature of the combat committed to by the United States—the defense of civilization against its enemies—gives it an open character, without a foreseeable end. For between

Islamist terrorism and the Western world, neither victory nor compromise is possible.

Thus we should get ready to live for a long time in this strange "state of war" against a poorly defined adversary. The purpose of this book is not to put U.S. strategy on trial, but rather to try to understand its deepest motivations, its real mechanisms, and most important its long-term consequences. For the reelection of George W. Bush gives the U.S. president the opportunity not only to change the United States but also to change the world, for better or for worse.

INTERPRETING THE BUSH
REVOLUTION

ƒ administration took office in January 2001, it had already adopted a strategy of breaking with the one that had preceded it. With its traditional view of international relations, it seemed prompted by a "Westphalian" conception of the world, in which the competition of sovereign states is the chief driving force of the international system. As summed up by two well-known analysts: "Bush and his advisers looked at the world in terms of states—whether great powers or rogue nations—not stateless actors."[1]

This tendency was expressed within the "Vulcans" group, Bush's original circle of advisers when he was a presidential candidate.[2] It was dominated by four personalities who shared a rather pessimistic and "Hobbesian" vision of the world: Richard Cheney, I. Lewis Libby (his main adviser), Richard Perle, and Paul Wolfowitz were already preoccupied at the time with the case of Iraq and the risks entailed in the proliferation of weapons of mass destruction.

The Republican elite was also obsessed by the idea of freeing itself from the yoke of international commitments made according to the principle of multilateralism, that is, constraints (freely agreed to) on the exercise of U.S. power for the benefit of the whole international community.[3] The protection of the United States' interests had to prevail over world responsibilities; hence the rejection of the traditional mechanisms of arms control as well as the distrust of the UN and the peacekeeping operations. This view was characteristic of the generation of men and women who came into power after the 1994 congressional elections. Since then, the majority tendency within the political class has been to regain freedom of action, which was viewed as seriously and unjustifiably diminished. Although U.S. reservations about the instruments of international law are often caricatured, the basic movement behind it is no less real, for it goes beyond the domain of the Bush presidency alone. In 2000, the Clinton administration had established a "Community of Democracies" in which some saw a possible alternative to the United Nations.

The overthrow of alliances in Eurasia, that is, the abandonment of the policy of partnership with Beijing in favor of a rapprochement with Moscow, had been a first concrete break. The U.S.-Russian summit of Ljubljana in June 2001 had cleared the way for a new entente between the two former enemies, particularly in the face of Islamic fundamentalism, already identified as a common adversary.

The other major axis of U.S. policy, related to the first, consisted of a reexamination of the country's energy strategy with a view to a diversification of imports. Probably the presence in high office of persons who had spent part of their career in the oil industry was influential in adopting this strategy. But the heart of the matter does not lie there. For several years, the energy situation had become worrying, given the simultaneous growth of consumption, dependence on foreign countries, and the price of gasoline. Between 1998 and 2001, the pump-price per gallon of gas had almost doubled, and expenses for energy per household increased by 25 percent. Since the end of the last decade, the United States had imported more than half the gasoline it consumes annually. The symbolic threshold of ten million imported barrels a day was exceeded for the first time in May 2003 and, according to projections, the United States will consume between twenty-five and thirty million barrels a day by 2030, while the national production will have diminished. In this context the growing Saudi autonomy as regards the setting of prices was judged worrisome. Energy security was a real priority for the Bush administration before September 11, and would have been so for any other president. During the 2000 electoral campaign Mr. Bush moreover had proven particularly attentive to the idea that America could be at the mercy of some foreign blackmailers for its consumption of oil.[4]

However, there was not yet anything revolutionary or messianic in U.S. policy until September 2001. Certainly, since the attacks of 1995 and 1996 in Saudi Arabia, the CIA had Al Qaeda in its line of sight. In 1996 Congress had voted a law authorizing military force against the infrastructures of international terrorism, and in 1998 Osama bin Laden was indicted by a U.S. court. During the same period, George Tenet, director of the CIA, had said that the intelligence community should consider itself "at war" with terrorism.[5] In 1999, Afghanistan had been ordered by the UN to end all support of Osama bin Laden.

But terrorism was only one of a number of threats to the United States, and was treated more as a law enforcement problem than as a national security problem. Bin Laden had been seen more as the banker of Al Qaeda than as the mastermind of international terror. U.S. strategy aimed to repress the Islamist nebula but not to destroy it;[6] terrorism could be "managed."[7] The image of a jihad against the American way of life was used figuratively, not literally.[8] Catastrophic terrorism was only a hypothesis of experts that didn't engage the attention of political leaders, with the exception of a few pessimists (like Vice-President Cheney).[9] The theme of a new Pearl Harbor was distinctly present in planning in defense circles, but defense was to be "electronic" or "spatial." There was no sign of the abrupt reorientation of U.S. strategy that was to come. The defense budget had been increased in 2001 only because of pressure from Congress. Mr. Bush was an avid follower of the "Powell doctrine" (clear mission, well-defined exit strategy) and had not clearly distinguished his policies from the policy of containment of the "rogue states": he had asserted that deterrence would remain the United States' first line of defense.[10] And though the new president had indeed claimed that the disarmament of Iraq was a necessity, he did not seem obsessed with a change of regime in Baghdad.[11]

Thus, the invasion of Iraq was not foreordained. Above all, it was not inevitable that a country formerly bound to abandon both Marx and Jesus—as a French author wrote in the 1970s— would find itself under the influence of an alliance between disillusioned Trotskyites and Christian evangelicals.[12] The events of September 2001 indeed made possible the coming to intellectual power of two potent political forces: messianic neoconservatism and southern fundamentalism.

MESSIANIC NEOCONSERVATISM

One of the most influential schools of thought in the U.S. political world today is made up of idealists wishing to renew a Reaganite world view—simple, optimistic, and based on the belief that America is an exception. Driven by two think tanks (the Project for a New American Century [PNAC] and the American Enterprise Institute [AEI]),[13] this movement counts on a new generation of conservatives in favor of an active engagement of the United States in the world.

Challenges to traditional conservatism regarding foreign policy had begun late in the 1940s, notably through the works of James Burnham, cofounder with William Buckley of the *National Review*. In two books, *The Struggle for the World* (1947) and *The Coming Defeat of Communism* (1950), Burnham had criticized the

doctrine of containment: the goal had to be liberation of the Soviet Union and overthrow of the Chinese communists. He had influenced the writing of the national security directives NSC-48
(1949) and NSC-81 (1950).

Modern neoconservatism was born of the personal development of Democrats who were inspired by liberalism (in the U.S.
sense, meaning originating in the left and sometimes the Trot-
skyite extreme left).[14] It was founded mostly by Jewish intellectuals who were ill at ease with the establishment-protesting,
hedonistic, and egalitarian culture of the 1960s; they were deeply
affected by the Israel-Arab war of 1967, and concerned about
greater firmness toward the Soviet Union.[15] Disappointed by the
Johnson and Carter presidencies, distrustful of the UN since the
1975 resolution describing Zionism as a form of racism, they had
formed the intellectual backbone of the presidential candidacy of
Ronald Reagan.

Domestically, the neoconservatives have condemned the ex-
cesses of the welfare state and liberalism, but particularly cultural
egalitarianism and the promotion of minorities. They have sought
to renew conservative thinking through the use of the language
and methods of the social sciences.[16] In the realm of foreign policy, they have rejected the two majority tendencies of the Republican Party (the realism of a Henry Kissinger and the isolationism
of a Pat Buchanan). Neoconservatism has been intellectually
shaped by such figures as Irving Kristol and Norman Podhoretz,
notably through the journals *The Public Interest* and *Commentary*.
Kristol, for whom a neoconservative is "a liberal who had been
mugged by reality," summarizes the foundations of the neoconservative doctrine as follows:

> First, patriotism is a natural and healthy sentiment and
> should be encouraged. . . . Second, world government

is a terrible idea since it can lead to world tyranny. . . .
Third, statesmen should, above all, have the ability to
distinguish friends from enemies. . . . Finally, for a
great power, the "national interest" is not a geographical term.[17]

The penetration of neoconservatism in the U.S. establishment
was carried out through two networks, one intellectual, the other
political. The tutelary figures of the intellectual theme have been
Albert Wohlstetter and William Van Cleave, one a mathematician,
the other a political scientist. Van Cleave, one of the driving forces
of the Committee on Present Danger, then a member of the National Security Council under Mr. Reagan, has mostly been a
mentor for many leaders of Donald Rumsfeld's Pentagon.
Wohlstetter's role was more important. He was one of the main in-
spirers of the United States' military strategy. His works have been
marked by the pursuit of invulnerability in the face of risks of surprise attack, and by the search for means of making the military
tool, even at the nuclear level, usable by military leaders. They are
largely responsible for calling into question two canons of U.S.
strategy since the early 1960s: stable deterrence through the acceptance of mutual vulnerability, and control of the arms race by international treaties. Wohlstetter never stopped "thinking about the
unthinkable"; his writings particularly emphasized overcoming the
dilemmas of nuclear strategy through "counterforce" options, antimissile defenses, and precise conventional means. With his col-
leagues at the Rand Corporation (notably Andrew Marshall, a
longtime key figure in the Pentagon who would become a close adviser to Mr. Rumsfeld), he inspired several tenets of the administration's strategies.[18] Fear of surprise attack, a central feature of
contemporary U.S. strategic culture, owes a great deal to the
Wohlstetter couple (his wife is the author of a classic book on Pearl

Harbor). He was also one of the first experts to worry about the risks of nuclear proliferation resulting from the spreading of technologies.[19] At the end of his life, he took a close interest in the Middle East and advocated the use of military force by coalitions of the willing to reestablish order and oppose dictatorships.

Though the man had no known political commitment, his career was consistent with that of the neoconservatives—from his brief youthful attraction to Trotskyism up to his defense, at the end of his life, of the use of military force against authoritarian regimes. One can add to the Wohlstetterian influence that of Paul Nitze and Fred Iklé, major intellectual figures of the U.S. strategic debate. The latter had been co-rappateur with Wohlstetter of the famous report *Discriminate Deterrence* that is still today an intellectual touchstone for the U.S. right.[20]

The political way was incarnated by two Democratic senators, Henry Jackson and Daniel Patrick Moynihan. Pro-Israel and very determined to free the United States from the shackles of arms control, Jackson had tried to federate this tendency around him with the Coalition for a Democratic Majority.[21] After him, his colleague Moynihan, one of the rare U.S. congressmen to have developed real intellectual reflection, had taken up the torchlight of neoconservatism in the Congress.

This antiestablishment vision was then opposed to the realism embodied by Henry Kissinger and, in a general way, to any policy that led to placing democracies and dictatorships on an equal footing. The tutelary figure of U.S. Realpolitik during the cold war was particularly loathed by the neoconservatives. Kissinger's vision of peace through balance of powers was radically opposed to their own, that of peace through moral consensus. It is true that the vision of this Spenglerian firmly convinced of the decline of the United States served as a foil for the partisans of a new U.S. century.[22] Starting in 1986, the neoconservatives had been

comforted in their hopes of promoting democracy by the changes
in the Philippines and South Korea.[23] At the same time, some of
the president's advisers (Elliott Abrams at the NSC, among them)
committed the United States to a policy of actively supporting resistance to communism.

The upsurge of neoconservatism in the U.S. decision-making
system happened at the time of the elections in 1994, which had
brought to power a new generation of Republicans under the
leadership of the party's short-lived great hope, Newt Gingrich.
The movement next organized with a view to presidential elections, beginning in 1996, notably with the creation the next year
of the PNAC.[24] This center is the most recent, the most media-
oriented, and the most influential conservative think tank today.
Its manifesto, published in 1996 by William Kristol, current
leader of the movement, and Robert Kagan, one of its principal
intellectuals, contained in embryonic form all the major theses of
the Bush presidency: refusal of the decline of U.S. power, a more
positive view of the military tool, end of the laxity toward dictatorships, moral clarity, and promotion of a benevolent U.S. hegemony.[25] It cited the famous document NSC-68 (1948), written
by Paul Nitze, who affirmed the necessity for America to maintain
military superiority in all fields. It was under the aegis of PNAC
that the neoconservatives prepared an open letter to President
Clinton in 1998, which ended up, in the form of the Iraq Liberation Act voted by the Congress, by making a regime change in
Baghdad an official objective of the U.S. policy. The letter had
been signed by some fifteen of the future leaders of the Bush administration or experts close to it.[26]

Even though the neoconservative movement initially supported the candidacy of John McCain, it later lined up behind
George W. Bush once the outcome of the primaries was estab-

lished, and it penetrated the administration through the game of the nominations with the self-interested support of Dick Cheney. But it was only after September 11 that neoconservatism asserted itself as a dominant political force in the U.S. decision-making system.

The name of the movement is in a certain way misleading: neoconservatives are in fact reactionary, when they seek to reaffirm old principles and to denounce the social and cultural reforms of the 1960s, or on the contrary revolutionary and even messianic when they seek to adapt the rules of the international society to new realities or to extend democracy on a global scale. Those of the neoconservatives who were inspired by Trotskyism naturally consider that revolution is possible: the Reaganite right willingly claims paternity for the "democratic revolution" in the East.[27] But in any event, neoconservatives are anything but conservatives.[28]

MYTHS AND REALITIES OF THE STRAUSSIAN INSPIRATION

The neoconservatives gladly invoke Winston Churchill, Andrew Jackson, or Ronald Reagan as models. But they also often embrace the teachings of two philosophers, Leo Strauss and one of his students, Allan Bloom of the University of Chicago. Both of them emphasized traditional moral virtues as opposed to relativism and egalitarianism, natural law against historicity, and classical philosophy against that of the Enlightenment.

Leo Strauss was inspired by the teachings of Socrates and Plato and by a return to the philosophical practice of the ancients. For him, the modern reformists and rationalists have undermined the foundational values of the West: virtue, reason, and civilization.

The vitality of Western culture lies in the interaction of and tension between its two great pillars, Athens (representing philosophy or reason) and Jerusalem (representing religion or revelation). A part of his work, the part that inspired the neoconservatives, concerns the question of democracy. Learning from the experience of the Weimar republic and Nazism, Strauss judged that the defense of the West against its enemies must be a moral obligation (he described the clash of the Islamic world and Christianity in the Middle Ages as an analogy to the fight against communism).[29] In the face of tyrannies, democracies cannot be weak, and compromise is impossible.

Strauss is thus among the writers who inspired the renaissance of U.S. conservatism in the 1950s. Having a different mentality from the dominant cultural model in American colleges and universities of the 1970s, his students turned toward the Republican circles, thus filling an intellectual vacuum, and many of them joined the Reagan administration before forming the framework of a conservative renewal.[30] But the philosopher's writings are now the object of an instrumentalization that leaves connoisseurs of contemporary philosophy perplexed and sometimes speechless. Certainly, Strauss's thought lends itself to various interpretations and his writings are not free of ambiguities. But it is only by over-interpreting the author's works that one would find the intellectual roots of the U.S. strategy: indeed, for the specialists, there is quite simply no Straussian political plan.[31] The philosopher only emphasizes the preservation of the national interest and social cohesion, and subordinates foreign policy to them.[32] Thus when critics of the administration exploit certain Straussian themes like that of the "noble lie" they go too far. Only a particularly fertile imagination could see this concept underpinning the formation in the Pentagon of the Office of Special Plans, dealing with the ques-

tion of weapons of mass destruction in Iraq, headed by the alleged Straussians William Luti and Abram Shulsky.[33] Irving Kristol, the founding father of neoconservatism, had some reservations
about Strauss, whose opposition to modernity and nostalgia for
the past he criticized. Michael Ledeen, one of the principal
thinkers of the war against terrorism, draws his inspiration from
Machiavelli, while Strauss preferred Aristotle (whom Irving Kristol considered the first nihilist). Albert Wohlstetter is said to have
been a disciple of Willard Van Orman Quine, a philosopher
whose thinking was opposed to that of Leo Strauss.[34] And the
neoconservatives' passionate defense of U.S. values was not a
characteristic feature of the philosopher.

In the extreme, however, it seems possible to say that Strauss's
somewhat cynical and egotistical vision in the area of foreign policy is reminiscent of the "Jacksonism" also claimed by the neoconservatives. The unilateral and defensive militarism of General
Jackson indeed seems to find a certain echo in Strauss's approach.
Didn't the latter suggest that "the only restraint in which the West
can put some confidence is the tyrant's fear of the West's immense
military power"?[35] The Straussians indeed gladly maintain that
dictatorships and rogue states work by different value systems
from those of the West.

For his part, Allan Bloom had a major influence on the thinking of the neoconservatives through his criticisms of cultural egalitarianism, the drifting of the U.S. educational system, and the
systematic promotion of minorities.[36] No foreign policy prescrip-
tions follow from his teachings. But commentators on U.S. politics may have underestimated the man's indirect importance.
Bloom was part of a distinct trend in the Straussian school inspired by Alexandre Kojève.[37] The latter saw in the U.S. experience a model for the satisfaction of human needs, one whose

superiority would be seen in the confrontation with the Soviet Union. Kojève started with the Hegelian theme of the end of history, but superimposed a Marxist analysis on it. He described the United States as a posthistorical model and predicted the victory of this model.[38] His reading of Hegel directly inspired the reflections of Francis Fukuyama, a disciple of Bloom, on the theme of "the end of history."[39]

These influences can be seen in U.S. policies through some key themes: the evocation of the 1930s in the neoconservative argument for the war in Iraq, Mr. Bush's frequent references to "moral clarity," his statement in the *National Security Strategy* of 2002 asserting that the twentieth century had seen the decisive victory of liberal democracy in the battle of ideas,[40] and his speech of November 2003 on the "global democratic revolution." In 1999 Mr. Bush had paid tribute to Ronald Reagan in affirming that there was in the world a "current," a "direction" in favor of democracy.[41] In 2004 Vice-President Cheney maintained that "the momentum of history is on the side of human freedom."[42]

Another intellectual thread should be mentioned, one connected with the preceding although not a school of thought, that has taken on new importance since September 11: those who are sometimes called Likudniks, unconditional supporters of the Israeli right wing. One of the distinctive features of the Bush administration has been the force of this movement within the civilian bureaucracy of the Department of Defense. It has available important points of support in Washington: the Jewish Institute of National Security Affairs and the Institute for Advanced Strategic and Political Studies, both of them unreservedly aligned with the positions of the Israeli right, as well as, to a lesser extent, the American Israel Public Affairs Committee and the Conference of Major Jewish Organizations, traditional champions of the cause of Israel in the U.S. political scene.

SOUTHERN FUNDAMENTALISM

Another major source of inspiration is the "culture of the South," the repository of a mythological legacy that consists of a set of premodern values inherited from the earliest colonists and from the conditions of the United States of America's birth. It is founded on the themes of religious persecution, social control by force in a hostile and dangerous environment, and a strict collective discipline aiming to protect itself from the external world. In its most extreme branches, its values are the superiority of the so-called white Anglo-Saxon race and regeneration through violence.[43]

But its religious dimension is probably the most significant for explaining current developments in U.S. politics. The membership of the principal political leaders in the established denominations (they are generally Methodists, Presbyterians, or Episcopalians) conceals the considerable importance of the evangelical inspiration in today's conservative elites. Evangelism became a dominant movement in America in the middle of the nineteenth century, and gave rise to other branches of Protestantism, such as Pentecostalism at the beginning of the next century. It was at this time that the term "fundamentalists" appeared, having entered everyday language around 1920, by contrast with "modernists." Its contemporary version appeared after the Second World War, splitting off from the Protestantism of the large traditional denominations, known as liberal. Having developed through mass preaching and the modern media, evangelism is notably embodied today in the Southern Baptist Convention, the largest Protestant church in the United States.[44] Representing at least 25 to 30 percent of the adult population (fifty to sixty million Americans), it is federated by the National Evangelical Association.[45]

The evangelical movement harbors a radical, politically active, and financially powerful tendency driven by a few key figures who are highly visible in the media: Jerry Falwell, founder of the defunct Moral Majority and once a spiritual adviser of Mr. Reagan; Pat Robertson, president of the Christian Coalition and of the Christian Broadcasting Network on television; Franklin Graham, who is close to Mr. Bush as his father Billy Graham was close to Nixon and the senior Bush, and in favor at the Pentagon;[46] Tim LaHaye, founder of the Council on National Policy, an organization that seeks to coordinate the strategy of the religious right, and the author of popular millenarian novels;[47] Hal Lindsey, author of very successful apocalyptic essays;[48] Jerry Vines, ex-president of the powerful Southern Baptist Convention; Robert Morey, president of the Faith Defenders; and Gary Bauer, president of the Family Research Council.

This school of thought advocates a literal reading of the Bible and declares the imminence of the end of times. Among its sources of inspiration is the strange doctrine of "dispensationalism," born in Texas in the nineteenth century and still taught today in the religious institutions of the Bible Belt (including the influential Dallas Theological Seminary). Its success is based on the fact that it breaks with the traditional postmillenarianism of Protestants: for it, the Second Coming will arrive before the thousand-year reign of Christ. To believe this doctrine of the *pre*millenarian kind, inspired notably by John Darby, we are currently living in the sixth and penultimate "dispensation," which will end in a seven-year war led by the Antichrist, and in the battle of Armageddon. It has as a result unconditional support for Israel, as the biblical prophecies can only come true if the Hebrew state is in possession of all the lands promised to it: hence the concept of "Christian Zionism" embodied in some militant organizations (including the International Fellowship of Christians and Jews, Christians for Israel, and Christian Action for Israel) whose success goes well beyond the evangelical movement alone, and that are federated by the National Unity Coalition for Israel, based in Kansas.

It is also inspired by an equally curious though more anecdotal Anglo-Israelism, born in Europe at the start of the nineteenth century. For this movement, the Anglo-Saxons are the direct descendants of the ten lost tribes of Israel, and their union with the Jews of the Holy Land would prefigure the Second Coming. The penetration of this doctrine into the United States in the late nineteenth century led to its splitting into several movements. One of them, moderate and low-key, has now returned to the ranks.[49] The other, extremist and appealing to lower classes, inspires the movement known as Christian Identity, to which are connected radical groups like Aryan Nations. The movement is a major ideological reference for the militias of the extreme right. For it, Israel should have remained British, whereas the Aryan race is the true chosen people.[50] This paranoid segment of rural America has become resistant to federal authority (and is against the United Nations or "world government"). That authority is alleged to seek the destruction of the traditional American way of life, and is called ZOG (Zionist Occupation Government).[51]

The evangelical denominations also vigorously promote creationism, a discipline seeking to demonstrate the historical truth of the Bible by contesting the Darwinian theory and mechanisms of evolution. In the past thirty years, creationism has become extremely influential in the U.S. educational system, with powerful college and university supporters working to give it scientific respectability.

When these "restoration theologians" entered into politics

three decades ago, they deliberately chose the tactic of renouncing the fatalism of traditional postmillenarians. The movement was expressed, notably, by the 1979 creation of the Moral Majority by Jerry Falwell, who had vigorously supported the candidacy of Ronald Reagan, and then by the 1989 establishment of the Christian Coalition by Pat Robertson and Ralph Reed, which incorporated evangelism in Republican circles of influence.[52]

The public for these ideas now goes far beyond that of fundamentalism itself (which represents only some 5 percent of the adult population and some 10 percent of the electorate). This success is explained by the development of American society during the second half of the twentieth century: the modernization of the South, the development of federal power, and the secularization of social institutions encouraged by the Supreme Court. Under Bush, the ultraconservative religious right has worked its way up to the highest level of political power, with men such as Attorney General John Ashcroft and Michael Gerson (the head presidential speechwriter). But its influence on Congress is perhaps the most striking, for it is of a nature to ensure political longevity. Among the elected representatives who can be linked to this sphere of influence are indeed the near-totality of the big names of the Republican Party (Dick Armey, Tom DeLay, Bill Frist, Dennis Hastert, and Trent Lott, among others).

It would be overdoing it to interpret U.S. strategy on the basis of religious convictions alone. The installation in the White House of a "born-again" evangelical Christian was not at all new: Jimmy Carter was a born-again Baptist, Ronald Reagan and several members of his administration were clearly inspired by millenarianism. But it can't be denied that the religious factor, seeking to give a spiritual dimension to combat, was among the primary motivations for entering a new kind of war. In this regard, the deep faith of the U.S. leaders reflects the steadfastness of the religious convictions of the population—a true exception among the highly industrialized countries.[53]

SEPTEMBER 11 AS A CATALYST

The events of September 2001 thus made possible the formation of a strange and powerful convergence of three distinct streams: the pessimistic but aggressive realism of a Cheney or a Rumsfeld, messianic neoconservatism, and southern fundamentalism.

These two trends were already well-represented within the Republican Party, which many Democrats had joined after the "treason" of President Johnson's legislation on civil rights. And the influence of the southern elites has considerably increased since the mid-1980s. But even so the party remained marked by a culture of government close to the traditional realistic school of thought.

September 11 acted like a catalyst for a new alliance that transformed the balance of powers in the U.S. right wing. Certainly, the complicity between neoconservatives and fundamentalists already existed at the time of Mr. Reagan, but to a lesser degree.[54] Mainly of a tactical order at the time, this connivance didn't have the same political consequences (for example, in the systematic support of Israel). And the southern culture hadn't yet become a major ideological component of the Republican Party. There were already personal connections between the neoconservatives and the party's aggressive realists, who worked together in the 1990s.[55] But going to war radically changed the situation. To describe this new convergence, the expressions "democratic imperialism" or "democratic realism" have been proposed.[56] It is also expressed in the strange phrase "balance of the powers to favor human freedom" proposed in President Bush's West Point speech, which was to become an essential axis of the security strategy of

2002 written by Condoleezza Rice, Steve Hadley, and Philip Zelikow.

This ideological alliance is in some respects surprising.[57] It was not foreordained that the traditional "Hobbesian" conservatives like Messrs. Cheney and Rumsfeld, and the prudent Ms. Rice, intellectually raised by party realists, would go along with idealistic neoconservatives like Messrs. Kristol and Kagan. The promotion of democracy by the neoconservatives is not exactly representative of U.S. southern culture. (In the 2000 primaries, the Christian right moreover had vigorously objected to their preferred candidate, Senator McCain.) Leo Strauss's love of Greek philosophy would be regarded with suspicion in southern colleges and universities, as would the exaltation of pagan or barbaric virtues dear to Theodore Roosevelt and now extolled in neoconservative circles. Above all, the intellectual Jewish neoconservatives of the East Coast and the Protestant fundamentalists of the South have radically different cultural and political views, and the religious right's support of Israel is not free of ambiguities. The Jews are destined to be converted or to ally themselves with the Antichrist. Though evangelicals of the most radical kind are theologically and politically Zionists, they are no less culturally anti-Semitic.[58] For the dispensationalists, if it was written that two-thirds of the Jews of Palestine must die, that must come to pass. It is thus not without reason that Michael Lind describes the grafting of the "head" of neoconservatism on the "body" of fundamentalism as an operation worthy of Frankenstein.[59]

For all that, this alliance is not merely one of convenience. Looked at closely, it involves a real convergence around a few essential themes: refusal of cultural relativism favoring instead intangible Western values, and contesting of dominant intellectual models in American colleges and universities; unapologetic references to the perennial fight between "good" and "evil" (some evangelical leaders have interpreted the "end of history" as meaning the "end of times"); respect for religion and its place in American society; return to a literal reading of ancient texts and distrust of the eighteenth-century rationalists and reformists; the sense of a mission to accomplish, without reluctance to use force; and the protection and defense of Israel.[60] In this regard, the common points between the Israeli sabra and the American pioneer could be cited: a heritage of conquering and a mentality of being besieged.[61]

Likewise, the alliance between the neoconservatives and the hawks like Cheney and Rumsfeld is based on common themes: during the cold war these two streams of thought were opposed to détente and arms control, as embodied by Kissinger. (Some of them played a role as links between the two streams, like former secretary of state George Shultz.)

The circles and organizations of the different persuasions identified above greatly overlap. It is under the aegis of the Institute for Advanced Strategic and Political Studies (Jerusalem and Washington), which openly promotes Strauss's theses, that the famous document *A Clean Break: A New Strategy for Securing the Realm* (1996) was produced by a work group headed by Richard Perle. The document suggested to the government of Benjamin Netanyahu that it abandon the Oslo process and that it adopt a policy of "rollback" towards Syria. Vice-President Cheney is not known to be a Straussian, but some of the people very close to him are, like his influential chief of staff, I. Lewis Libby, or his wife, Lynne Cheney.[62] Moreover, at the Pentagon, nerve center of America at war, all the dominant intellectual leanings of the U.S. right wing are found: disciples of Strauss, defenders of Israel, and admirers of Franklin Graham. And the Rand Corporation, one of the favorite think tanks of the Department of Defense, has been the privileged background of numerous influential persons in the administration.[63]

At the center of these networks, one finds three of the most intellectually influential individuals in the Bush administration: Vice-President Cheney; Richard Perle, until 2004 an adviser of Mr. Rumsfeld and nicknamed the "prince of darkness";[64] and Paul Wolfowitz, deputy secretary of defense. Wolfowitz has the twofold trait of having been directly exposed to the influence of such major figures as Allan Bloom and Albert Wohlstetter, also Fred Iklé, Paul Nitze, and George Shultz; and of sponsoring such influential personalities as Francis Fukuyama, Steve Hadley, I. Lewis Libby, and Zalmay Khalilzad.[65]

THE IDENTIFICATION OF EVIL

When the first major attack on U.S. territory since 1812 occurred, the shock of 2001 was utterly intolerable for the neoconservatives, who wished that the United States would fully exercise its freedom of action; but the shock also made possible America's moral and military rearmament of which they had dreamed—in the image of the turning point of 1950, when North Korea's invasion made possible adoption of a strategy of containment.

As in the cold war, civilization is supposedly once again threatened by a "totalitarian" ideology.[66] As in the Civil War or the great world conflicts, the United States considers it is facing up to an "existential" threat.[67] The struggle against terrorism is thus likened to a "fourth world war," to use the now famous expression of Eliot Cohen, a military expert close to the neoconservatives (though proposed as early as 1992, as we have seen, by Alexandre de Marenches).[68] Through its geographical extent, it warranted the name of world war (Osama bin Laden's messages moreover justified these terms, evoking a fight carried on "in Palestine, Iraq, Chechnya, Kashmir, the Philippines, and Afghanistan").[69] Through its historical scope, it would fall under the same category as the preceding great conflicts. And its ideological bases would not be so far from those characterizing the two preceding world conflicts: the Islamists would be seen as defending a totalitarian kind of world view; as for Iraq's and Syria's Baath parties, it is recalled that they had been inspired by the NDSAP (German Workers Party), hence the constant references to the SS and the Holocaust, the KGB and the Kominterm, which characterize the neoconservative literature, and the frequently used expression "Islamofascism."[70]

In the end, however, it is "evil" that is the alleged enemy. The United States has indeed gone to war inspired by a moral vision resting on a striking syllogism: America has been attacked, *hence* freedom and civilization have been attacked, *hence* the enemy can only be evil itself. On the evening of September 11, Mr. Bush declared, "Today our nation saw evil."[71] At the funeral oration given at the National Cathedral in Washington three days after the attacks, he declared, "Just three days removed from these events, Americans do not yet have the distance of history. But our responsibility to history is already clear: to answer these attacks and rid the world of evil."[72]

Mr. Bush did not have to go against his true nature to use this vocabulary. During his first presidential campaign, hadn't he asserted "the Empire has passed, but Evil remains"?[73] The expression "axis of evil" was thus perfectly revealing of the administration's way of thinking: it was Michael Gerson, head presidential speech writer and a strong evangelical, who had transformed the phrase "axis of hatred" first proposed by his team into "axis of evil."[74] This return to moral simplifications, religiously inspired, was well received by a large part of the U.S. population and its elites. It is, in the strict sense of the word, reactionary:

> After years and years of substituting therapeutic lan-
> guage for moral language, "well" for "good," "ill" for
> "evil," Americans seem sick of therapy. They long for
> good old-fashioned "evil." Looking at the hole where
> the World Trade Center stood, they see—"evil."[75]

Particularly representative of this vision was the speech delivered by President Bush to the cadets of West Point on June 1,
2002, a true founding of what was later called the Bush doctrine,
announcing a break with decades of "deterrence" and "containment," that is, coexistence with the adversary. It is probably the
one that neoconservatives best identify with:

> . . . moral clarity was essential to our victory in the
> cold war. . . . Different circumstances require different
> methods, but not different moralities. Moral truth is
> the same in every culture, in every time, and in every
> place.[76]

Going to war also made possible a process of identifying with
Israel, and the support of that country is plain in public opinion.[77]
If Europeans could feel themselves "all Americans" on September
11 (headline in the daily *Le Monde* the day after the attacks), the
Americans discovered they themselves were "all Israelis." This
identification was not self-evident beforehand. Certainly, Americans have long been sympathetic to the Hebrew state, and the
U.S. political mythology has always included a biblical connota-
tion, the founding fathers having seen the country as a new
Jerusalem.[78] And the 1967 Israel-Arab war saw emerge a tremen-
dous wave of fellow-feeling among the Democrats who were later
known as neoconservatives, as well as among Protestant fundamentalists. But Israel has never been an ally in the military sense; it

has been backed up by Washington only since 1973, and some Republican presidents have been very tough with Israel. Mr. Bush's team took over command with a favorable bias toward the Hebrew state, but without any political plan for it other than moving the U.S. embassy from Tel Aviv to Jerusalem. Henceforth the two nations are said to be facing the same threats (terrorism, proliferation, dictatorships), and they respond to them in the same way (preemptive acts, antimissile defenses, political assassinations). And never was the United States so supportive of Israeli policy, even in its most disputed features.

This strategic convergence assumed a sacred dimension for the Republican right wing. Two peoples considered the chosen ones in the U.S. tradition, the Anglo-Saxons and the Jews, henceforth face the same dangers; two religions, evangelism and Judaism, henceforth share the same enemy. The fight against Islamist terrorism has taken on a literally eschatological meaning. For many Americans, it is indeed no less than the battle of Armageddon that has begun. It is a matter of, as it were, delayed-action millenarism: the attack on the Pentagon and the Twin Towers in New York would be the sign that had been vainly awaited at the turn of the century.

September 11 thus gave a spiritual meaning to U.S. policy, and Mr. Bush is said to be convinced of the religious meaning of his mission.[79] His speeches are sprinkled with biblical references, often implicit and meant for the initiated.[80] Quoting the prophet Ezekiel, he reportedly affirmed at the end of 2003 the risk of seeing Gog and Magog rush from Babylon into Israel.[81]

Unrivaled but also without an overall plan since the fall of the Soviet Union, America now found a "vision" again. The attacks of September 2001 made it possible to channel a political, economic, and military force that had no clear reason for being: it was, as one commentator remarked some months previously, "all pumped up," but with "nowhere to go."[82]

They also gave a poorly elected president an overarching political goal. The war against terrorism was not launched for electoral reasons, but it is clear that the White House strategy seeks to store up its political benefits. It is not Karl Rove, the president's chief political adviser, who decided to make war in Iraq; but it was desirable for the operation to be concluded before the 2004 electoral campaign began. Two categories of voters were considered particularly important to the Republicans. First, the evangelical Christians who represent about 20 percent of the electorate: of the fifty million Americans who voted for Mr. Bush, Karl Rove estimated that fourteen million were evangelicals, and that there was a "reservoir" of four to five million voters in this category who didn't vote in 2000.[83] Next, the Jewish voters who traditionally do not vote for Republicans but whose support might be useful in disputed states. The domestic political dynamics are thus a factor strengthening the most radical features of the U.S. strategy, and Bush's reelection proved that Mr. Rove's strategy was right.

In the U.S. system there are mechanisms for cushioning the impact of extremist forces that appear in political settings. During the whole period from 2001 to 2004, the Pentagon was a considerable orienting force whose influence went well beyond its theoretical responsibilities; but the State Department and above all the team of the National Security Council, whose role is coordinating U.S. foreign policy, often curbed the fervor of the neoconservatives.[84] (Conversely, the neoconservatives have criticized the administration's policy toward China and its support of authoritarian regimes like Saudi Arabia, as well as the Pentagon's mistakes in preparing for and carrying out of operations in Iraq.)[85] And President Bush himself, whose personal authority was considerably strengthened by his change into commander in chief of the war, did not systematically adopt the ideas developed by Messrs. Perle and Wolfowitz.[86]

This moderating role had only limited effect, for Ms. Rice has been more of a personal adviser to the president than the orchestrator of U.S. strategy (besides the fact that her team included leaders who favored neoconservative choices).[87] Moreover, the very personality of the administration's most reasonable elements, like Colin Powell, limited their ability to confront those conventionally called hawks.

With Ms. Rice in charge of the Department of State and Mr. Hadley in charge of the National Security Council, one may expect a more coherent foreign and security policy—but not necessarily a turning back on the first mandate's orientations.

2

WAGING THE FOURTH WORLD WAR

IS THERE A coherent strategy for implementing these objectives? Many tend to imagine U.S. policy as the outcome of a long-term vision, a preestablished plan, and a perfect coordination of the persons involved. The reality is much more prosaic. The political structure of the United States (strict separation of the executive and the legislative powers, elections every two years, influence of interest groups) in fact makes it—perhaps more than any other Western democracy—subject to piloting by eye, improvisations, and changes of course. Its implementation often consists of short-term decisions resulting from the objective interests of the moment: the U.S. logic is more often empirical than imperial. What was true before September 11 largely remains so today. However, the particular characteristics of the current period make it possible to determine more easily than in normal times certain lines of force in U.S. strategy that are henceforth powerfully rooted in the country's political culture and will not disappear for a long time.

TERRORISM, TECHNOLOGIES, AND TYRANNIES

The policy followed after September 11 was very quickly described as a "global war on terror." This is no traditional conflict: in many respects it is a postmodern war. It targets networks more than states. It calls on intelligence, police, and justice more than on military means. It has an important economic and financial dimension.[1] And it is also, perhaps above all, ideological. The propaganda in favor of democracy and U.S. values holds an important place in it. The United States has announced its intention to increase radio broadcasts in Arabic and Farsi and to double the budget of the National Endowment for Democracy, and it has launched an ambitious "Initiative for the Broader Middle East" to aid in transforming the area's societies.

The struggle undertaken by the United States consists first of an attempt to reduce the immediate threat, the international terrorist networks. "Our war against terror begins with Al Qaeda, but it does not end there. It will not end until every terrorist group of global reach has been found, stopped, and defeated."[2] These groups are cited on an official list of thirty-six organizations, the majority of them Islamic. Straightaway, moreover, the war has been enlarged to include local organizations without any "global reach."[3] Didn't Mr. Rumsfeld suggest a few hours after the attack on September 11, "Go massive. Sweep it all up. Things related and not"?[4]

Very quickly, the war was extended to states knowingly sheltering such terrorist networks, where, if necessary, a change of regime would be brought about. On September 11 Bush declared, "We will make no distinction between the terrorists who committed these acts and those who harbor them."[5] Some days later he expressed an essential principle of the "Bush doctrine": "From this day forward, any nation that continues to harbor or support terrorism will be regarded by the United States as a hostile regime."[6]

Thus, by extension, the war against terrorism had also become a war against states supporting terrorism, and also against states having weapons of mass destruction or being capable of transferring such instruments to terrorist groups.[7] The attack on the

World Trade Center immediately led strategists to realize that the destruction of September 11 was nothing compared to what would be caused by the explosion of a small nuclear weapon in the center of a large U.S. city. Some days later, the anthrax crisis abruptly showed the vulnerability of Western societies to a biological attack, even one of very weak magnitude. The risk of a nuclear, biological, or chemical attack was known: it was now plausible. The proliferation of weapons said to be capable of mass destruction was seen as dangerous: it was now unacceptable. For a respected analyst in conservative circles, "The greatest threat facing us—and one of the greatest ever to threaten mankind—is the collision of this collective fantasy world of Islam with the horrendous reality of weapons of mass destruction."[8] The publication during the winter of 2002–2003 of the *National Strategy to Combat Terrorism* and the *National Strategy to Combat Weapons of Mass Destruction* was the practical translation of the organization of U.S. strategy around these two axes. Hence a cardinal principle of the Bush strategy: "Any outlaw regime that has ties to terrorist groups and seeks or possesses weapons of mass destruction is a grave danger to the civilized world—and will be confronted."[9] Thus, in only a few months, what was initially a "war against terrorism" had become a "global war on terror."

The war was also to be an operation meant to create fear and respect. Inspired by Middle East specialists such as Bernard Lewis and Fouad Ajami, conservative ideologists such as Norman Podhoretz and James Woolsey have sought to demonstrate that America had to go to war to once again be respected, notably by the Muslim world. According to them, the United States was attacked in 2001 for the same reason that it had been in 1941, because it had given its potential enemies an image of weakness; and likewise in 1980 (failure to free the hostages in Iran), 1983 (withdrawal of the marines from Lebanon),[10] 1988 (attack above Lockerbie),

1991 (ceasefire against Iraq), 1993 (withdrawal from Somalia, attack on the World Trade Center), and in 1998 (attacks at Dar es Salaam and Nairobi).[11] The U.S. authorities took up this theme.[12] The neoconservative commentators said out loud what the White House was probably thinking quietly: the interventions in Afghanistan and in Iraq also had the goal of "dispelling the myth of U.S. weakness" and "restoring a healthy fear of U.S. power."[13]

Beyond this dimension, U.S. strategy also reflects a global political plan. The United States believes it ought to spread democracy not only to protect itself ("Democracies do not make war on each other"),[14] but also because it fits in with the very nature of American society. Here the hypothesis of a "fourth world war" becomes convincing. In 1917 Woodrow Wilson wanted not only to defend civilization, but also "to make the world safe for democracy."[15] In 1941 Roosevelt had warned, "we will not only defend ourselves to the uttermost but will make very certain that this form of treachery shall never endanger us again."[16] Three years later the fight had become "a mighty endeavor, a struggle to preserve our Republic, our religion, and our civilization, and to set free a suffering humanity."[17] (Churchill himself spoke of a fight for "Christian civilization.")

The United States has again linked up with this theme of an historic mission. In 2001 Bush announced, "In our grief and anger we have found our mission and our moment. Freedom and fear are at war. The advance of human freedom . . . now depends on us."[18] This discourse was extended on November 6, 2003, promising a "global democratic revolution," extending to a worldwide scale the political plan of Mr. Reagan during the cold war: encouraging the fall of authoritarian regimes and favoring the dawning of democracy.[19] Along with it, the rivalries of the great powers would be put to an end.[20]

The war against terrorism, which has already turned into a war against weapons of mass destruction, has thus become a war against dictatorship. This speeding up of history seems to suit the neoconservatives. It is true that neoconservatism was defined in the past as a form of "Trotskyism in reverse" with the ambition of exporting democracy and not revolution.[21] The war thus becomes a fight to promote liberal democracy, the only legitimate form of government, of which the United States is the most successful incarnation. America thus seems to want to remake the world in its image.

In the writings of some intellectual conservatives, this aspect assumed epic proportions. For the philosopher Lee Harris, the U.S. wager is nothing less than "the only possible escape from the kind of historical impasse or deadlock in which the human race presently finds itself."[22] And for historian Andrew Roberts, "The English-speaking peoples' alliance . . . is the last, best hope for mankind."[23]

The idea of reorganizing the international environment is not unique to Republicans. It corresponds to an old tradition, one that has often been supported by Democrats, from Woodrow Wilson to Bill Clinton. (Clinton's national security adviser, Anthony Lake, had called this the strategy of enlarging market democracy.) But here it is a matter of enlarging by force and of overthrowing authoritarian regimes by military action. Wilson attempted to forge a new international order based on law and collective security; for his part, Clinton counted on trade to bring peoples together, and on sanctions to resolve the problem of rogue states. Hence the expression "Wilsonism in boots" suggested by Pierre Hassner to describe Mr. Bush's policy, or the description by two American authors of neoconservatism as "a new political animal born of an unlikely mating of humanitarian liberalism and brute force."[24]

The "rogue states" are the first order of concern. This category was not invented by the Bush administration. For some decades, the United States has kept lists of countries identified as supporting terrorism or developing weapons of mass destruction.[25] When one compares these lists, which have changed very little over time, five countries show up that can be considered central to U.S. obsessions since the end of the cold war: North Korea, Iraq, Iran, Libya, and Syria. This "Club MAD," to use an expression of a Bush administration official, does not include the group of countries that have remained outside the nonproliferation treaties: the legal criterion is not essential for the United States.[26] But the five states are located at the crossroads of tyranny, technology, and terrorism, according to a formula that is popular in Washington.[27] The break consists of a change of policy toward them: coexistence with such regimes is now judged impossible. The United States "can no longer allow that the world's worst weapons are in the hands of the world's worst regimes."[28] (Even though it currently doesn't have nuclear, chemical, or biological weapons, Saudi Arabia is increasingly often added to this list by analysts close to the administration.)

The first three, presented in January 2002 as representative of an "axis of evil," then shared certain features: they were authoritarian regimes maintaining or suspected of maintaining weapons of mass destruction programs, and supporting terrorism or having supported terrorism in the past. All three had been especially branded by the Clinton administration and by the presidential platform of then-governor Bush as states likely to have the capacity, at the start of the twenty-first century, to threaten U.S. territory with ballistic missiles.[29]

The expression was maladroit, for these three states were in different situations. The case of Iraq was unique. To American eyes, no other country in the world presented the political and symbolic stakes found in Saddam Hussein's Iraq. Regime change in Tehran and in Pyongyang was not an official goal of U.S. policy.[30] But Iran itself was also a special case compared to the two others. Indeed, Iraq and North Korea had been central to U.S. military policy since the end of the cold war: under Clinton the military implement had been redesigned to make it possible to confront, if necessary, two simultaneous regional conflicts, according to the accepted way of expressing it: one new war triggered by Iraq and a North Korean invasion of the peninsula. Moreover, what these two countries had in common was that they were still legally at war with the United States. The White House also wanted to avoid giving the sense that a war against Iraq was imminent, and didn't want to single this country out.[31] It was essentially for circumstantial reasons that Iran was placed alongside Iraq and North Korea. At the start of 2002, Iran had been suspected of sheltering some leaders of Al Qaeda who were on the run, and the affair of the *Karin-A* (a boat transporting arms to Palestinian territories) had sparked the fury of the Bush administration . . . which had decided to send Tehran a strong message.

Nevertheless, more was attributed to the expression "axis of evil" than it signified.[32] The three countries concerned were indeed mentioned only by way of example: the U.S. president's exact terms were "States like these, and their terrorist allies, constitute an axis of evil, arming to threaten the peace of the world."[33] Above all, the expression was intended only as a political label and not the statement of a doctrine, and it disappeared from official vocabulary as quickly as it was introduced into it. By the spring, it was indeed no longer used, neither in its form (the expression itself) nor in its substance (the list of the three countries), and it is thus wrong to continue to present it as central to U.S. strategy. In the *National Security Strategy of the United States* published a few months after the president's speech, only Iraq and North Korea were named.

In 2004, a new goal was announced: to avoid the seizing of power in a state with weapons of mass destruction (Pakistan) or vast oil reserves (Iraq, Saudi Arabia) by extremist individuals or groups who would then be in a position to attack the West.[34]

Finally, one finds again, in a less explicit way, the "realist" tendency of U.S. strategy: preventing the resurgence of a power capable of standing up to the United States. This vision finds its roots in an effort between 1990 and 1992 under the aegis of Richard Cheney, then the secretary of defense, by a team including the principal instigators of Mr. Bush's policy. The vision was to serve as the basis for planning U.S. defense up to the end of the century.[35] It was also present in the platform of the PNAC for the defense policy of the United States in 2000, which recognized that such a strategy would be hard to bring into play "absent some catastrophic and catalyzing event—like a new Pearl Harbor."[36] The *National Security Strategy* contained numerous elements representative of this "realist" conception of the world. But it described as a goal the benign model (one which, all things considered, was not far from the concept of multipolarity defended by others) of a "world where great powers compete in peace" and a "balance of power that favors freedom."[37] The neoconservatives themselves saw further yet, and some of them fully approved the prospect of a worldwide imperium.

The Bush administration's strategy thus had the peculiar characteristic of being as much concerned with states that are *too weak,* that poorly control their territory and are vulnerable to extremism, as concerned with states that are *too strong,* able to defy the United States. It delineated the contours of a reassuring return to a Westphalian form of order in which the states are the main agents of world politics.[38]

It is useful to say a word about oil, which, according to many commentators, is supposed to be the ultima ratio of U.S. strategy. However, the claim that the harnessing of hydrocarbons from the Middle East and central Asia by U.S. industry is one of the essential determinants of the administration's strategy hardly withstands analysis. The majority of U.S. imports of oil (50 percent) comes from the western hemisphere (Canada, Mexico, Venezuela) and only about 20 percent comes from the Persian Gulf. Saudi Arabia is the number two supplier of oil to the United States but accounts for less than 10 percent of the country's consumption.[39] And if it were merely a matter of making Iraq a partner to counterbalance the Saudi influence on the oil market, the lifting of sanctions against Iraq would have been a much simpler and less costly means. Although the Texans of the Bush administration could probably not cut themselves off totally from the interests of the great oil companies, to suggest that these companies were able to impose their agenda on the presidency was hardly serious: in the past one has seen many examples of differences between the strategies of the oil tycoons and those of political leaders.[40] The energy security sought by the United States is achieved first and foremost through the diversification of the sources of energy and supplying countries, notably on the American continent itself and in Eurasia. The goal is not to control Gulf oil, but to avoid hostile Islamist regimes able to resort to economic blackmail of Washington.

RETURN TO FORCE, PURIFICATION OF ALLIANCES

As regards implementation, the U.S. strategy consists in a "return to the use of force," accompanied by a reorganization of alliances and change from a strategy of containment and deterrence to one of roll-back and preemption.

The lifting of constraints and inhibitions on the use of armed force is a clear break from the past: elimination of the ban on the CIA resorting to political assassination (which had probably prevented it from getting rid of bin Laden), rejection of the half-measures of the Clinton era such as limited strikes with cruise missiles, and an end to excessive restrictions on committing personnel (what has sometimes been called the preoccupation of "zero death").[41] The return to force is accompanied by a reaffirmation of the *arma cedant togae* principle.[42] It is the political authorities, not the armies, still reputed to be overcautious, that must control the course of the war and have the last word.[43] Hence a real regaining of control over the Pentagon by civilian leaders, and a leading role for personalities like Paul Wolfowitz, and also Douglas Feith, Steve Cambone, and Dov Zakheim. It was in a sense foreseeable that the Bush administration was inclined to the militarization of its international policy: hadn't all the administration's principal figures, with the exception of Ms. Rice, served in the Pentagon at some point in their careers?

At the same time, the military tool was revitalized through a considerable increase in the defense budget, which rose to its average level during the cold war, and to the transformation of the army's operational modes, which until September 11 had come up against the conservatism of the Pentagon. The idea, inspired notably by Andrew Marshall, was to take advantage of technological progress to develop new concepts for the use of force, by emphasizing in particular precision strikes and real-time intelligence. (Richard Perle has described Operation Iraqi Freedom as the first Wohlstetterian war.)[44] Another major innovation was the considerable increase in the role of special forces.[45]

The return to force was of course a result of September 11. It corresponds to an idea long cherished by many in the Republican Party. It had been promoted by the Western Republicans in the

1950s (the so-called Asia Firsters), and it had been partly implemented during Mr. Reagan's term of office (Afghanistan, Grenada). But this concept is easier to apply now, for during the cold war its partisans were rebutted by the risk of a global conflict.[46]

Initially, priority was given to counterterrorism operations in Afghanistan. The operation against Iraq meant the opening of the second phase of the war, with potential targets being the authoritarian regimes holding or assumed to be holding weapons of mass destruction. For William Kristol, the overthrow of Saddam Hussein was only the "end of the beginning" of the war.[47] The thinking about Iran and Syria is primarily justified by the security of Israel; that about North Korea is based on the risk of seeing nuclear technology sold to other states and to terrorist groups.

It is in this context that one must read the growing indifference of the United States vis-à-vis formal multilateral systems, which are seen as unduly imposing constraints on the exercise of U.S. power and unduly applied equally to all states, whatever their political regime. NATO is criticized as cumbersome: its decisions are made by consensus, the voice of the United States weighing as much as the others. Arms control and nonproliferation treaties are deemed useless at best, and dangerous at worst: allegedly, it is not so much the arms that are bad than it is that those who use them are badly intentioned.[48] The argument is close to the one used by the very conservative National Rifle Association to oppose legislation limiting bearing of weapons: "Guns don't kill people; people kill people." And those treaties are said to be unfavorable to democracies, for democracies are said to sign their commitments in good faith, unlike dictatorships.

According to this view, the United Nations is at best powerless and at worst threatening. The organization unifies the opposition: the fundamentalists who do not hesitate to denounce the prospect of a "world government";[49] American southerners who take a poor view of any interference of a higher political authority in their affairs;[50] and the pro-Israeli circle of influence, who have distrusted it since the 1975 resolution that labeled Zionism as a form of racism. Beyond that, the United States finds it harder and harder to accept the presence of states such as Syria in the Security Council, the chairmanship by Libya of the Human Rights Commission (or the exclusion of the United States from the same commission, as occurred some years ago), or the memberships of Iraq, Iran, and North Korea in the Committee on Disarmament. The presence of these countries in international organizations by the same right as democracies is henceforth considered unacceptable by most of the U.S. political establishment.

It is thus the very principle of collective security as implemented in the twentieth century that is called into question. Alone acceptable in the eyes of Washington are the groups of democracies dominated by the United States like the G8, or at the limit, the Atlantic Alliance in its political arm (for the neoconservatives, a decision of NATO would be as legitimate as a mandate of the UN). On the other hand, the Community of Democracies founded in 2000 receives their favorable attention.[51] Here the name "new Wilsonism" is misleading, for we are far from the system that President Wilson sought to set up just after the First World War. The precedent of the League of Nations, to which the United States never belonged, reminds us that the U.S. distrust of a multilateral system it doesn't control is a sentiment that goes way back.

U.S. alliances have entered a period of profound reorganization. Just after September 11 began what has been rightly called the "purification of alliances."[52] Whoever was not with the United States was with the terrorists.[53] This process of reorganization led Washington to move away from the permanent multilateral alliances in favor of old bilateral alliances and "coalitions of the willing." This model, which had been introduced in the first Gulf War (with a UN mandate at the time) now seems established as a general rule. NATO was left out of the main operations in Afghanistan and Iraq, but old alliances in Asia got a new lease on life for the benefit of the war against terrorism. It also led the United States to get closer to countries rightly or wrongly considering terrorism a threat to their very existence, like India, Israel, and Russia, and to revive, as during the great ordeals of the last century, a policy of tactical alliance with some authoritarian regimes. Hence the surprising cooperation with countries traditionally condemned by Washington, like Sudan, or with undemocratic countries, like Uzbekistan. The worldwide coalition against terrorism is in fact the widest in history: 134 countries offered their assistance to the United States after September 11, and ninety took part in one way or another in Operation Enduring Freedom (twenty-seven of them in Afghanistan itself).[54]

One year after the war in Iraq, this logic had not been abandoned, and Mr. Bush asserted, "There is no neutral ground—no neutral ground—in the fight between civilization and terror, because there is no neutral ground between good and evil, freedom and slavery, and life and death."[55]

But this process of purification lies mostly in the rebuilding of a hard core formed by countries with Anglo-Saxon culture that have long cooperated closely in the field of intelligence: the United States, the United Kingdom, and Australia, the main military actors in operations Enduring Freedom and Iraqi Freedom. This return to the alliance between English-speaking peoples against the common enemy and for freedom was greeted with enthusiasm by non-U.S. figures like Conrad Black, David Frum, and Andrew Roberts (cited above).[56] This somewhat unexpected dimension of the war was, it is true, promoted by a convergence of circumstances: first, the fact that both the British and Australian prime ministers shared a certain moral view of policy and a readiness to use force for this purpose (Tony Blair has sometimes been compared to Churchill by the neoconservatives), and were eager to strengthen bonds with Washington; next, the fact that America could count on the support of the two great media empires of Rupert Murdoch and Conrad Black.[57] This probably shouldn't be given excessive importance: Canada and New Zealand were opposed to the war, and some of America's best allies in the Iraqi adventure, like Spain and Poland, were of a very different culture. In fact, there were in each of them certain predispositions to get closer to America, whether it was a matter of the gratitude of countries recently liberated from dictatorship, or of the importance of the terrorist problem in their recent history, or of the religiosity of their leaders.

More important is the unwavering nature of the Bush-Blair partnership. The United Kingdom certainly had good reasons to get directly involved in the war: its past of colonial power in the area, its status as America's unfailing partner in all the operations against Iraq between 1991 and 2003, its experience in the struggle against terrorism, as well as perhaps its indirect responsibilities in the development of Islamism in Europe (the country having long been a haven of tolerance for extremism). But the roots of the British commitment were deeper: Mr. Blair indeed embodied an old moral tradition in the Labor Party, which at its start was largely dominated by evangelical Christians. Strong cultural ties have long existed between the Freemasonic and religious communities in the two countries.[58]

PREVENTION OR PREEMPTION?

The strategic rupture announced by George W. Bush in June 2002, and presented by commentators as a doctrine of preventive war, has probably been exaggerated. This description must be relativized in many respects. First, it was a matter of *preemption*, a concept different from *prevention* where the threat is supposed to be already present, serious, and immediate—it was a matter of shooting first, as in the era of pistol duels in America's old West. The logic is supposed to come under legitimate self-defense, and to be underpinned by legal reasoning inspired by Hugo Grotius or Thomas More.[59] Next, there was no question of giving up the policy of deterrence, but rather of confronting its limits in the face of states that might not be responsive to the threat of reprisals against their territory, and in the face of nonstate actors that by nature cannot be the object of such threats.[60] Preemption was meant to be just an option—a possible choice and not a doctrine. As Bush administration officials have repeatedly said, "different threats require different strategies." It was to be employed only as a last resort, as soon as the risks of inaction, from the U.S. point of view, exceeded those of action.[61] Finally, one should note that the concepts of preventive and preemptive operations were already part of U.S. strategy: the preventive destruction of opposing nuclear arsenals was considered several times, whether of the Soviet Union, China, or even North Korea; and preemption was already among the strategic options of counterterrorism under Mr. Clinton.[62]

It remains true that the emphasis on preemptive options has bought the U.S. strategy closer to that of Israel, which several times in its history conducted military operations presented as coming under this category. The destruction of the Osiraq nuclear reactor in 1981, condemned at the time, is now presented as a model in Washington. The ambiguity of U.S. policy lies in the fact that what had been presented as *preemptive* war with Iraq was in fact a *preventive* war. There was obviously no serious and immediate threat by Iraq to U.S. interests: even the most hardened neoconservatives had recognized it before the results of the UN inspections.[63] But they also maintained, as did the administration itself, that the new forms of threat made necessary the adaptation of the law: while in the past an army massed at the borders made it possible to announce the imminence of an attack, terrorist groups don't necessarily give such clear signals ("When was 9/11 imminent?"). As Mr. Rumsfeld later explained, "We acted because we saw the existing evidence in a new light, through the prism of our experience on September 11."[64]

In this framework, the deployment of defenses against a limited ballistic attack, requested by the Republican majority in Congress since the mid-nineties and accepted only reluctantly by President Clinton, is henceforth an integral part of the U.S. strategy. Here again it is a matter of completing deterrence by a guarantee of last resort in case of failure. The main motivation, strengthened by September 11, is to avoid being blackmailed or subjected to political pressure by a state armed with long-range ballistic weaponry, as North Korea, Iran, or Pakistan might be in the next ten years. The antimissile defenses are also conceived as a tool to prevent ballistic proliferation: if the United States protects itself, its potential adversaries would be less tempted to invest in such instruments. Here one finds the U.S. wish to dissuade any country with the ambition to confront it in a military competition. The spectacular increase in the defense budget since 2002 also follows from this logic.

THE SPIRIT OF EISENHOWER

The precedent of Pearl Harbor has often been mentioned in connection with September 11, and the irony of history had it that Messrs. Cheney, Rumsfeld, and Wolfowitz—long obsessed by the theme of the "strategic surprise"—were in charge of the U.S. military machine that day. In the 1980s, Cheney and Rumsfeld also took part personally in exercises known as "Continuity of Government," intended to test the reactions of the administrative apparatus in case of a nuclear attack.[65] And a few weeks before September 11, Paul Wolfowitz had told the U.S. Army cadets, "Surprise happens so often that it's surprising that we are still surprised by it."[66]

But there the parallel ends. Mr. Bush was not as close to committing America to the war as Mr. Roosevelt had been after the attack by the Japanese. And, for the United States, the attack of 2001 was much more serious than that of 1941.[67] The reference to the years 1948–1950 (the Berlin blockade, the first Soviet nuclear explosion, the North Korean invasion) is probably just as relevant. From the U.S. point of view, the first decade of the twenty-first century seems to be a reflection of that time. Sketched between the lines in the writings and speeches, a face from history begins to emerge: that of John Foster Dulles, the secretary of state from 1953 to 1959, a Christian conservative who was opposed to containment and to negotiation with dictatorships and who advocated instead rollback and America's moral and military rearmament.[68] Dulles, at the time an adviser to Truman, had been among those who insured that rollback became an option of U.S. strategy by 1949–1950. Here some have seen the influence of James Burnham (see chapter 1), who has sometimes been retrospectively called "the first neoconservative."

Consciously or not, the themes and vocabulary of the start of the cold war were updated in line with current taste: the U.S. rhetoric henceforth fell into place around a few key formulas taken directly from the language of that earlier time: "with us or against us,"[69] "don't wait for threats to materialize before fighting them," "at a time and in a way of our choosing."

It has been aptly said that the presidency of Ronald Reagan was a source of inspiration for that of Mr. Bush, and neoconservatism sometimes likes to call itself neo-Reaganism. The famous speech of June 8, 1982, before the House of Commons in London on the universality of democratic values was a touchstone for the Bush administration. The principal promoter of this theme at the time was Elliott Abrams, whom we find again at Mr. Bush's White House, first responsible for democracy and human rights, then from December 2002 on, for the Middle East. (He had also had a part, under Mr. Reagan, in the rapprochement between the Jewish community and the Christian right.)[70] Similarly, the speech of March 8, 1983, before the National Evangelical Association on "the evil empire" served as an inspiration for Mr. Bush. Further, the 1986 raid against Libya was one of the rare U.S. military counterattacks on terrorism. Finally, the theme of dissuasion recalls the "competitive strategies" of the Reagan era: the Pentagon is tempted to apply to China the strategy that is supposed to have worked with the Soviet Union.

But there are few points in common between the former governor of California, whose traditional evangelism left room for a fierce defense of individual liberties and who hesitated to act when his counselors were not in agreement, and the former governor of Texas, inspired by more modern forms of Protestantism, who is commanding when dealing with his cabinet. By the same token, one can hardly forget that despite the temptation to use force, Mr. Reagan's presidency was marked by a certain reserve in the actual use of the military: it was in this era that the Weinberger doctrine was formulated (that will later reemerge in the form of the Powell doctrine), articulating the strict conditions for a recourse to arms. His defense of democracy was essentially motivated by the fight against communism. It was only in 1986 that the administration started to support the democratization of allied countries in Asia and Latin America. Finally, Mr. Reagan did not display the same support of Israel as has Mr. Bush.

Though other historical references to the present time could be brought forward, such as John Quincy Adams, Theodore Roosevelt, or Andrew Jackson, the real point of reference of President Bush seems in fact to be Dwight D. Eisenhower, and the U.S. strategy basically appears to be a true flashback to the earliest years of the cold war: restructuring of alliances; shifting from containment to rollback and from deterrence to preemption; involvement of the United States in the Middle East (the Eisenhower doctrine, which at the time had already created the impression of a fight against Islam); and references to the fight between "good" and "evil."[71] The fear of a nuclear attack on the U.S. capital moreover led the country's leaders to reactivate programs of civil defense and "Continuity of Government" inherited from the beginnings of the American-Soviet confrontation.

This similarity between the Bush and Eisenhower presidencies has not been widely noticed. However, from the start, the Bush presidency had strange similarities to that of his illustrious predecessor: a belief in the promise of nuclear energy, America's resolute commitment in favor of Taiwan, and a reaffirmation of the religious character of America.[72] It is a tradition for each entering president to choose a portrait of one of his predecessors to display in the White House: Mr. Bush chose President Eisenhower.[73] No doubt the early identification of Mr. Bush with his predecessor, another combatant president, was strengthened by September 11 and by his reelection in 2004.

3

THE WORLD AS A
THEATER OF OPERATIONS

THE EXTENT OF the operation against Iraq has obscured the diversity of military actions conducted in the war against terrorism, by means that have ranged from mere technical support (Indonesia), to major operations (Afghanistan), and direct assistance (the Philippines, Georgia, Somalia), to occasional raids (Yemen). In 2004, more than 350,000 Americans were stationed around the world, including 250,000 engaged in operations.[1]

But the geostrategic developments presently underway go well beyond military operations alone. World geography as seen from Washington is indeed undergoing a major change, historic in scope and commensurate with the objectives described in chapter 2; September 11 accelerated the process.

For Hegel, the wind of history blew from east to west. For America, history seems to be written in the opposite direction: centered in the nineteenth century on the western hemisphere, then in the twentieth century on Europe, the U.S. strategy seems to be focusing on Asia in the twenty-first. Modifications of permanent deployments had begun at the start of the 1990s with a rebalancing under Clinton between the two continents (100,000 men on each side). Europe, which had been central to U.S. strategy since 1917, has been called to move to the background. As a continent, it is perceived as a pacified theater; as an actor, it is seen as a fractious partner with inadequate military capabilities. Hence the progressive diverting of the U.S. strategy to an area stretching from the Maghreb to the Far East.

A profound transformation of the U.S. military deployment is beginning to emerge. The system set up after the Second World War—a huge presence at the two extremities of Eurasia to hold back the Soviet giant and ward off a resurgence of German and Japanese military nationalisms—has had its day. The U.S. bases are to be smaller in the future to avoid their leaving an excessive political imprint, and to allow for their dispersion, with a more homogeneous geographical distribution. According to the "Global Posture Review" unveiled in September 2004, the importance of "main operating bases" is to be reduced in favor of "forward operating sites" and "cooperative security locations."[2] Some sixty to seventy thousand personnel are to be relocated to the United States in the coming decade. The new deployment pattern, called "lily pads," aims to make possible the rapid projection of forces in case of crisis, with the help of numerous local relays. New points of support are thus envisaged in Europe (Bulgaria, Poland, Romania), the Middle East (Iraq, Qatar), central Asia (Kyrgyzstan, Tajikistan, Uzbekistan), Africa (Djibouti, São Tomé), and in the Asian Pacific area (Australia, Malaysia, the Philippines, Singapore, Thailand).

Although the surveillance of oil wells and pipelines is not the primary role of the GIs, the search for greater energy security is nevertheless tied to this strategy. One of the motivations behind the new relationship between Moscow and Washington is thus the energy partnership reached by the two countries (the joint exploitation of deposits of hydrocarbons, strengthening of the network of oil and gas pipelines). Energy security also entails the diversifying of sources of the supply, in the Middle East, and also in Africa, Asia, and Latin America.

The analysis of the new U.S. strategic geography can be broken down into several major regional groupings: the Middle East, the peripheral areas of the developing world, Eurasia, and finally China, which deserves separate discussion.

THE MIDDLE EAST, OR
THE CRUX OF THE PROBLEM

Since the end of the 1970s, the Middle East has gradually become, for the United States, the center of the strategic world. The military headquarters overseeing this region is aptly named CENT-COM (Central Command), with an area of responsibility from Egypt to Pakistan.[3] The distinctive feature of this region is that it presents a veritable catalog of U.S. obsessions: terrorism, weapons of mass destruction, oil resources, illegitimate dictatorships, and Israel's security. Four of the five countries traditionally presented as the main adversaries of the United States are found in this area.

The U.S. strategy in the region since 2002 seems to be clear: crush the potential threat from Iraq and then resolve the Palestinian issue. Pursuing these goals, Washington hoped not only to stamp out a potential threat to the United States and Israel, but also to take away any legitimacy from the war announced by bin Laden, whose stated goals are the end of "the occupation of the holy places" (the U.S. presence in Saudi Arabia since 1990 and Israel's sovereignty over Jerusalem), and the defense of the Palestinian cause.

As is well known, this strategy now goes beyond mere threat reduction and envisages a real re-creation of the Middle East. The idea was inspired by a few conservative intellectuals like William Kristol, Bernard Lewis, and David Horowitz. Inspired by some of these advisers, and indirectly by Lewis, President Bush has formed the conviction that the United States could no longer defend the status quo in the Middle East.[4] Lewis explains that the local elites' failure to construct modern states has created a resentment of English-speaking nations, which are seen as usurpers of power in the region. The main causes of failures in the Islamic world are said to be authoritarianism and lack of freedom.[5] The

Middle East was thus characterized as "a dysfunctional region that needs shock therapy," to quote an influential adviser to President Bush in January 2002. The heralds of the democratic revolution note that half (twenty-three exactly) of the world's forty-five dictatorships are in the Middle East.[6]

The operation against Iraq was desired by many leaders of the Bush administration at the time it took office, but it wouldn't have been possible without September 11. Was it inevitable after the attacks in New York and Washington? It seems that Mr. Bush entertained the hypothesis of an action against Baghdad at the end of 2001, but that his determination to act was built up only very gradually during 2002.[7] On February 16 of that year, Mr. Bush had signed a directive on Iraq that confirmed the goal of an overthrow of the regime.[8] But the idea of decisive action didn't really take shape until the beginning of the summer.[9]

Operation Iraqi Freedom was supposed to be the first site of a gigantic operation of geostrategic engineering. It was to be not only the second major military battle of the war on terror, but also the driving force of a reconstruction of the region on the basis of four new facts: the end of Iraq's moral and financial support of Palestinian terrorism;[10] the disappearance of a state-supported threat to the security of Israel, and the interruption of a chain of proliferation from the Mediterranean to the Sea of Japan; the possibility that U.S. forces could then leave Saudi Arabia and at the same time have available a new strong point for containment of Iran and also Syria;[11] and the supposedly exemplary nature of the future democracy in Iraq for the rest of the Arab world.

This last point, a sort of dominos-in-reverse theory, was, as is well known, essential to U.S. thinking. The question of weapons of mass destruction was a matter of real concern, and the head of the CIA had assured the presidency that the case was strong.[12] But the question had been put forward essentially for reasons that were legal (it was the subject of existing resolutions of the United Nations) and political (it was the only grounds on which all the members of the administration were in accord).[13] For the White House, Iraq had to be to the Middle East in the 2000s what Spain had been to Latin America in the 1970s and what Poland was to Eastern Europe in the 1980s.[14] For the neoconservatives, "promoting democracy in the Middle East is not a question of national egotism. It has become a question of national well-being and even of survival. On September 11, the problems of the Arab world became our own problems."[15] This logic was affirmed by President Bush in a speech at the American Enterprise Institute on February 26, 2003.

The intervention in Iraq also had, much more than the war in Afghanistan, a cathartic power. One can say that it was the symbolic revenge for September 11 (not unlike the 1983 Grenada operation following the Beirut bombings). Saddam Hussein had been the only head of state to publicly rejoice after the New York and Washington attacks. For the U.S. population and its elites, he was the perfect embodiment of the face of evil. An attack on the symbolic Babylon was met with a response on the real Babylon. Indeed, during the fall of Baghdad, the book of Isaiah and its references to the "fallen statues in Babylon" was copiously quoted in Washington.[16] More seriously, the idea of sending a message to all the potential adversaries of the United States was probably a more or less conscious part of U.S. motivation.[17] In any case, for the partisans of the war, the result is that "now our enemies know us better, and respect us more."[18] This is what writer Paul Berman has called a "Nixonian" reason.[19]

Oil was probably not an essential reason for the intervention in Iraq. The United States already had considerable access to Iraq's oil under Saddam Hussein's regime, and if it had been a matter of investing in Iraq's production capacities, the lifting of sanctions would have been less costly and less risky (including for the oil market). But the risk of one day seeing a Saddam try to seize the Saudi Arabian oil fields was probably still a part of the U.S. calculation, as it had been in 1991.[20]

It was indeed in the Greater Middle East that the main geopolitical game was supposed to be played, for it was there that the conjunction of authoritarian regimes, terrorist networks, and weapons of mass destruction was to be found, and it is there that the concerns of various U.S. players converged.[21] For the neoconservatives, the initial targets were precise: Al Qaeda, Iraq, and the Hizbollah.[22] But from that point on, they went further, like James Woolsey, who identified the goal as the elimination of the threat represented by the Sunni Islamists.[23] To this list of priority targets, they also often add Hamas and the Islamic jihad, considered largely responsible for the deteriorating situation in the Near East.

In the Persian Gulf, it is obviously Saudi Arabia that is at the core of this thinking. That country is now paying for the Faustian bargain it once made with the Islamist movements, which it financed for decades, disregarding the cost, provided there was peace in its territory. The Saudis had not foreseen the radicalization of the Wahhabi fighters in the Afghan melting pot.

The place of the kingdom in U.S. policy has become the subject of a real debate in Washington, as the majority of terrorists who caused the attacks of 2001 carried Saudi passports. There was some consensus on the plan to weaken Riyadh by making it lose its centrality in OPEC but some prospective ideas go much further. During a briefing before the Defense Policy Board, at the invitation of its president Richard Perle, Laurent Murawiec, an analyst from the Rand Corporation, created a scandal by saying aloud what many administration officials were thinking privately:

Saudi Arabia was the heart of the problem.[24] For Francis Fukuyama, it was largely responsible for the rise of "Islamo-fascism" in
Muslim societies.[25] The idea of using force to break up the Saudi
power was born out of the first oil shock in the 1970s.[26] Today it
is a major part of the thinking in neoconservative circles, taking
the form in the most extreme cases of plans for carving up the
kingdom's territory.[27]

For the time being, it is only a matter of "separating petro-
dollars from Wahhabism," that is, preventing oil income from financing, directly or indirectly, terrorist networks in the Middle
East and Asia, notably through charity organizations.[28] Washington will also do its best to approach head-on with its ally the question of the place of Wahhabism in Saudi society, which experts
close to the administration judge to be at the heart of the problem
of reforming Islam.[29] Certainly trouble was already brewing in
the alliance of the two countries before the attacks of September
2001, as Saudi Arabia showed growing independence of U.S.
policy (including the setting of oil prices). As early as summer
2001, Prince Abdallah had reportedly urged Washington to force
Tel Aviv to end its military actions against the Palestinians, other-
wise the kingdom would put an end to its alliance with the United
States.[30] But given the close ties between Washington and
Riyadh, any serious reconsideration of policy will be difficult and
painful.

The United States is also paying increasing attention to the
United Arab Emirates. That country, which had been alone with
Saudi Arabia and Pakistan in recognizing the Taliban regime, has
proven to be the nerve center for financing terrorism, and also, as
is known since the revelations concerning Pakistani nuclear traf-
ficking, for facilitating nuclear proliferation.

The other U.S. Middle East is centered on Israel. Here, Syria is key. The only immediate neighbor of the Hebrew state that has not normalized relations with it, Syria has long been suspected by Western analysts of having developed a chemical arsenal and continues to support certain terrorist networks. The question of whether Syria and Lebanon should be the target of military action has become the subject of a debate in Washington (the Pentagon's enthusiasm having been curbed by the CIA, which judges cooperation with Damascus to be valuable). Moreover, the future of Egypt—traditionally a regional power and long-allied with the United States, but also a cradle of modern Islamic fundamentalism—is arousing, albeit softly voiced, questions. As for Jordan, it is one of the only countries in the region to find favor with Americans—to the point that some people would gladly see the Hashemite sovereignty restored in the holy lands, which Churchill, a hero of the neoconservatives, had wanted to maintain.

The United States has not forgotten northern Africa, where the question of terrorism is the focus of current analyses. The U-turn in Libyan policy has been a pleasant surprise, which Washington now shows as an example for other rogue states to follow. As for Algeria and Morocco, they are the object of more sustained attention, both as targets of terrorism and as centers of new, violent movements.

The U.S. path in the Middle East is strewn with uncertainties. Obviously, the occupation of Iraq was badly prepared for (the Department of State had been kept out of it by the Pentagon), and the extent of the task of reconstruction was underestimated. The claim that democracy would prove contagious is just an incantation for now—a voodoo geopolitics, by analogy to the "voodoo economics" of President Reagan.[31] Intoxicated by their "victory" in Europe, the neoconservatives had perhaps forgotten that the domino effect of democratization in the 1990s had been possible only because of the domination of one key country over all the others: nothing of the kind exists in the Middle East. Finally, the administration's goals are contested by some of its best ideological allies: the principle of allocating territory for the formation of a Palestinian state runs counter to evangelical thinking.

In any case, despite the wishes of certain neoconservative experts ready to attack Syria or Iran, the Iraq adventure will probably remain unique, for it was possible only because of the special place that country holds in U.S. political mythology (besides the fact that operations of this magnitude are of a nature to mobilize most of the country's ground forces). But essential questions remain unanswered. Can Saudi Arabia be abandoned at the risk of bringing about its radicalization? Must Syria be punished for its arms programs or should it be praised for its cooperation in the struggle against Al Qaeda? Should every effort be made to hasten the counterrevolution in Iran, at the risk of an anti-U.S. backlash?

Indeed, at the heart of the debates is the U.S. policy toward Tehran. William Kristol judges that the neoconservative wager and the future of the war against terrorism lie there.[32] Many believe that Iraq, where the holy cities of Najaf and Karbala are found, can now compete with Iran as the center of the Shi'a world, and can usefully contain that country, which is still regarded as a potential threat. Now suspected by Western countries of developing nuclear weapons, Iran largely financed and supported terrorism in the Near East, and is supposed to harbor leaders of Al Qaeda. Other thinkers—foremost among them neoconservatives, obsessed with Iran since 1979—judge on the contrary that that country is ripe for a new revolution and that a modern Iran, freed of the grip of the clergy, could take the place of Saudi Arabia and become again a privileged ally of the United States, as well as a model for the Islamic world. Ideally, it would become a new Turkey, a country viewed with admiration by the neoconservatives (at least before the Iraq war).

One possible strategy in case of failures in the process of democratic pacification in the Middle East would consist in changing politico-religious alliances: while in the last few decades Sunni Islam had been a de facto ally of America, the abandonment of Saudi Arabia could lead to a rapprochement with Shi'a Islam, making its two beacon countries, Iran and Iraq, new allies of the United States. This strategy would be consistent with the idea of breaking up Saudi Arabia, where some oil fields are situated in areas with a Shi'a majority.[33] It would take advantage of the fact that the Shi'a are despised by a large part of the Sunni terrorists. Could Shi'a Islam be the ally of a U.S. power inspired by the evangelical right wing? At first glance, this idea may seem far-fetched. But certain analysts have noted strange similarities between the two cultures: Puritanism, as much as Shi'ism, places value on redemption through suffering, strict community discipline aiming to protect against evil from the outside, and a Manichean conception of the world—the origins of which can be traced back to Zoroastrianism.[34] The Iranian revolution had moreover certain points in common with the American Revolution.[35] The accord of these two politico-religious trends is a hypothesis at least as credible as that of their conflict.

In this game, the nuclear problem will certainly be a key factor. Those in Washington who want to restore friendly terms with the former Iranian ally are ready to pass over in silence possible violations of the Treaty of Nonproliferation of Nuclear Weapons; others judge on the contrary that the possibility of a compromise with the Iran of the mullahs is all the more difficult as that country could well be, in a few years, the only country not to admit the existence of Israel while at the same time possessing the capacity to physically destroy the Hebrew state.

FRONT LINES AND
PERIPHERAL THEATERS

The rest of the developing world (Africa, Latin America, Southeast Asia) has several common features from the U.S. point of view: it presents numerous examples of "failed" or "collapsed" states that can turn into centers of terrorism or refuges for it; it includes large areas of friction between Christian and Muslim communities; it is favored territory for U.S. evangelical movements; and it holds abundant reserves of hydrocarbons.

In Africa the states that command attention foremost are those capable of giving shelter to terrorist networks (Nigeria, Somalia, Sudan, Yemen, etc.), and to a lesser extent the oil-producing countries (Angola, Guinea, Nigeria, São Tomé, Chad, etc.). Already very present militarily in Djibouti with 1,600 personnel, the United States is seeking new bases in the Horn of Africa and in the Gulf of Guinea. Within the scope of a "Pan-Sahelian Initiative," U.S. special forces have been sent into the Sahara (Mauritania, Chad, Mali, Niger), officially for training in antiterrorist operations.[36] The continent's northeast is no doubt one of the world's regions in which counterterrorism operations will be the most significant. Africa, long neglected by U.S. administrations and analysts, has been the object of increasingly sustained attention, particularly with respect to its politics and religion, as the proselytism of the evangelicals attempts to slow down the expansion of Islam.

In Southeast Asia the strategy relies first on the Philippines, with which the United States has a long-standing treaty of alliance (as it does with Thailand), and where 1,100 military personnel have been deployed for counterterrorism operations. But it is Indonesia, the largest Muslim country in the world, an immense fragmented country ("our own Balkans," according to one U.S. admiral) subject to terrorism, which is no doubt at the center of U.S. preoccupations in the area; its natural resources also command attention. In an area with 206 million Muslims (95 percent in Indonesia and Malaysia) there is a fear that certain regions or islands of Southeast Asia are becoming sanctuaries of Al Qaeda and its affiliates. The size of forces permanently stationed in Korea and Japan will be reduced, probably in favor of the presence in the Pacific (Guam, Hawaii). The United States planned to withdraw a third (12,500) of the 37,000 Americans in South Korea before December 2005.[37] Finally, Latin America, a traditional domain of U.S. interest, has not been left out of current concerns. Certain areas considered sanctuaries for terrorists attract attention, like the region known as the Triple Frontier (Argentina, Brazil, Paraguay), which, it is said, could become a new Libya, that is, a meeting place and common ground for exchanges of views by terrorist movements of various ideologies.[38] And President Bush wishes to considerably increase the share of Mexican oil in U.S. imports (less than 10 percent right now). For the rest, the usual fixation points remain: the Castro regime, Venezuelan oil, and Colombian cocaine.

For its part, Eurasia has seen its position transformed on the U.S. geopolitical chessboard. It is there that the changes have been most profound, and it is there that one of the main frontlines of the global war on terror is located. For, beyond the criticisms that have been raised against the operation in Iraq, the whole of the Eurasian mass is on the side of the United States in the war against terrorism. It's what Charles Krauthammer has called "hyper-unipolarity," stressing "no single great power on the planet lies on the wrong side of the new divide."[39]

The process of democratization in Eastern Europe and the enlargement of the Atlantic Alliance have led to a considerable expansion of U.S. influence on the continent. One third of U.S. forces stationed in Europe are to be withdrawn. The number of U.S. forces stationed in Germany (71,000 today) will be reduced by more than half.[40] Heavy forces will be relocated to the United States, others will be "forward-deployed" to southeastern Europe. The end of the Russian ideological ambitions and the necessity of managing the immense nuclear inheritance of the Soviet Union had already brought Moscow and Washington together. But the Western choice of Vladimir Putin, his determination to fight against Islam, and the abundance of the country's reserves in hydrocarbons, have led to making Russia, no longer an adversary, a quasi-ally of the United States. Whereas Sunni fighters had been the favored partners of Washington to contain Soviet ambitions on its "southern balcony" during the cold war, Mr. Putin benefited from a true windfall: Russia could present all forms of repression of Chechen separatism as a part of the international war on terror. As a pledge of alliance at the end of 2001, Moscow reached an important and little-noted decision: it withdrew its last two overseas bases, the listening post of Lourdes (Cuba) and the naval base of Cam Ranh (Vietnam). This partnership has fostered an unprecedented cooperation between the two former adversaries on the edges of Russia, from the Caucasus to the border with China.

The United States is henceforth present in central Asia for the long term, and has extended its military presence there with bases in Afghanistan, in Kyrgyzstan (Manas), and above all in Uzbekistan (Khanabad). The latter country, with which a treaty of alliance and cooperation was signed at the end of 2001, is seen as a future regional power that will be able to have a part in stabilizing a region that remains, around Afghanistan, one of the main potential centers of Islamist terrorism. Beyond that, the U.S. presence in central Asia is seen by some as a means of holding back a possible resurgence of Russia.

Another geopolitical upheaval, perhaps less spectacular but just as important, has taken place in southern Asia. While the United States was gradually growing closer to India since the end of the cold war, along with the growing integration of that country in the international economy, September 11 led Washington to renew its ties to Pakistan, which had been strained since 1990. At the same time, New Delhi sought, like Moscow and Beijing, to benefit from the opportunity to justify its own efforts to combat Islamist terrorism.

But these three great powers allied with the United States in the war against terrorism cannot be put on the same level in U.S. strategy. China is indeed a special case whose strategic importance goes far beyond the war against terrorism. The People's Republic has long been one of U.S. conservatives' bêtes noires, and many of them see it someday taking the place once held by the Soviet Union, that of principal enemy—enemy certainly of a different nature, for it is driven by nationalism and the wish to be recognized as a great power, more than by a political ideology with a universal calling; but an enemy that is just as dangerous through its economic and, increasingly, military power. The "peer competitor" feared by Messrs. Cheney and Wolfowitz as early as 1992 would not be a reemerging Russia, but a China that is developed, modern, and nationalistic.

The theme of the threat from China rose in power in the U.S. political debate during the 1990s. Two developments contributed to it: on one hand, the increase in the trade deficit (a tenfold increase from 1988 to 1995); on the other hand, the development of Chinese thought caused by the Tiananmen Square revolt, the Gulf War, and the end of the USSR, which it is said led Beijing to increase its military budget and begin an accelerated modernization of its armed forces. Then a radicalization of tensions between the two countries took place with the crisis of the Straits of Taiwan (1996), the strengthening of the Japanese-U.S. alliance (1997), and the bombing of the Chinese Embassy in Belgrade (1999).

Starting in the mid-1990s, analyses appeared that renewed the theme of the "Chinese threat" (which had disappeared at the end of the 1950s), but featuring two very different perspectives. One of them is of a "realist" nature: it rests on the observation of a contradiction between the Chinese goal of hegemony in Asia and the U.S. goal of a balance of power in the region.[41] According to this view, China's ambitions are prompted by nationalism fueled by historical humiliations and grandeur thwarted by the West. The country would develop into a corporatist, militarized state not unlike Franco's Spain or Mussolini's Italy. This vision lays stress on the regional dimension of Chinese power and Beijing's growing influence on surrounding nations. The military modernization of the People's Republic would have the goal of preventing domination of Asia by a single power—except for China itself, whose goal would thus be to become the continent's tutelary power. The other vision is ideological: it reflects a moral combat very close to that of the neoconservatives.[42] Between the lines, it repeats the themes and codes of the U.S.-Soviet confrontation, and constructs a "global" Chinese threat in the image of the Soviet Union during the cold war. Far from becoming more democratic, China would seek to replace Moscow at the head of a new communist and subversive international organization, supporting movements and regimes opposed to U.S. power. There would be a consistent strategy on the part of Beijing aiming to increase its forward bases in the western hemisphere (Cuba, Venezuela, Panama).[43]

The U.S. debate about which strategy to adopt toward the People's Republic recalls the debate during the cold war in connection with U.S.-Soviet relations. The ideologists harshly criticized the traditional Republican policy inspired by Henry Kissinger, every bit as much as they condemned the "engagement" practiced by Mr. Clinton with regard to Beijing (which in 1995 had explicitly rejected the "containment" of China). Conversely, the realists are opposed to the policy of containment, which they judge doomed to failure. They reason that China is harder to "manage" than the Soviet Union, for the latter was a military power on a failing economic base while the former is an economic power whose armed forces are rapidly expanding.

While refusing to meet Beijing head on, Mr. Bush took up his post wanting to delineate his difference from his predecessor and announced that the People's Republic would be considered a potential "strategic rival," using the expression coined by the expert David Shambaugh.[44] The incident at Hainan (April 2001), where a U.S. reconnaissance plane made an emergency landing on Chinese soil after being targeted by a fighter plane of the PRC, was followed by a U.S. recommitment to the defense of Taiwan. Was this an act of U.S. provocation? The hypothesis is tempting, but it seems that was not the case. In December 2000, right in a period of transition between two presidential terms of office, the United States had already complained of the attitude of Chinese pilots who seemed to be seeking a confrontation.[45] On the other hand, the U.S. attitude during the crisis of 2001 had hardened only when Beijing had chosen to dramatize the incident.[46] One should note that the EP-3 spy planes had to fly low and thus relatively close to the Chinese coastline because of their mode of propulsion.[47]

In any event, it indeed seems that the relations between Washington and Beijing were on a collision course. This debate was interrupted by September 11. During the first summit with Jiang Zemin, George W. Bush stated that he had chosen cooperation over confrontation, and let Mr. Jiang know that it was up to Beijing to make an identical choice. The logic corresponded to what Zalmay Khalilzad had called, before becoming part of the administration, "congagement," a middle way between containment and engagement.[48] So, for the time being, China is a partner in the war against terrorism, but tomorrow?

4

THE TRAP:
AMERICA ENSNARED?

MUST THE U.S. strategy be condemned? Considering the scope of the risk of terrorism, it is not certain that the status quo in the Middle East would have been preferable. The incantations about the need to maintain the "stability" of this region have become increasingly irrelevant with the rise of terrorism: stability has become deadly. The neoconservatives have had no trouble disparaging the apparent tolerance of their opponents for the worst regimes on the planet. And if the awkward expression "axis of evil" was rightly criticized, nevertheless it has to be recognized that technical and military cooperation between authoritarian regimes is a reality.[1]

The U.S. policy has triggered positive developments. The terrorist movements are now severely suppressed in Pakistan and Saudi Arabia. Since 2002 the countries of the Middle East have taken first steps of political reforms that are at least partly attributable to pressures from the West: elections in Bahrain, adoption of a new constitution in Qatar, reform of the conditions for naturalization in Egypt, appointment of a commission of human rights and reform of family law in Morocco, and a promise by the Gulf states to reform religious education. And though the dynamics of the conflict between Israel and the Palestinians remain unchanged, a few significant developments have occurred since 2001 (proposals of Prince Abdallah, adoption of the "road map," appointment of a Palestinian prime minister).

Furthermore, the war against terrorism itself has produced real results. In 2004, some 70 percent of the known leaders of Al Qaeda were allegedly inoperative (including Khalid Sheik Muhammad, its "head of operations").[2] Between two thousand and thirty-five hundred militants of the circle of influence were said to have been killed or captured.[3] According to one respected analyst, the organization itself was reduced by 80 percent and the number of its members is now less than one thousand; more than one hundred terrorist attacks have been avoided.[4] Some $200 million in terrorist assets have been frozen or seized.[5] Saudi Arabia closed the Al-Haramain Foundation, which was suspected of playing an indirect role in the financing of Islamist terrorism. Neither Afghanistan nor Iraq can serve any longer as a sanctuary or a base for the terrorist networks. And there has been an unexpected effect of the war: Al Qaeda and its affiliates contributed to the delegitimation of resorting to armed violence by certain separatist or independence movements.[6] Iran, Sudan, and Syria seem to have settled down, probably in part out of a fear of U.S. intervention.[7] The prohibited activities of Iraq were not as advanced as thought before the war; but in any case the country no longer presents a potential danger. Libya's renunciation of its weapons of mass destruction is probably, in part, due to the warlike attitude of the United States and its allies. (The same is true of Sudan.) Finally, the Proliferation Security Initiative has helped to bring to light the nuclear trafficking conducted by the Pakistani Abdul Qadeer Khan. The Pentagon's policy in Iraq was perhaps a failure, but the neoconservatives have always said that it would be a long task ("ten years" according to one of the leaders of the movement). The situation in Iraq in 2004 was in many ways comparable to the situation in Germany, Japan, or South Korea in 1946. It is much too early to make a definitive judgment about the success or failure of the U.S. wager in the Middle East. In any case, as Donald Rumsfeld said candidly in an internal memorandum in October 2003, the work of the coalition in Afghanistan and in Iraq will remain for a long time a "long, hard slog."[8]

It is certainly tempting to dwell at length on the U.S. Army's and Marine Corps' difficulties on the ground. The Pentagon itself had focused on the war and had pushed the Department of State away from the operation of administration and reconstruction (even though diplomats had devoted a considerable amount of time preparing the occupation).[9] According to UN officials, it had underestimated the strength of Iraqi nationalism and had given excessive importance to the differentiation between the Sunnis, the Shi'a, and the Kurds. At the same time, it had overestimated the capability of the local elites to form an alternative to Saddam Hussein's regime—there was no political entity constituted on the spot when the U.S. troops arrived. From the promotion of Ahmed Chalabi and his Iraqi National Congress (a group of dubious exiled Iraqis with little local credibility) to the hasty preparation of a UN resolution leading to the total abandonment of the country's sovereignty (Resolution 1483, May 2003), America's choices were seen as at best erroneous and at worst humiliating. And the breakup of the Iraqi army is considered by all the experts to have been a grave error. The United States was forced to strip the Korean peninsula of thirty-six hundred military personnel in order to cope with the deterioration of security and the defection of certain allied contingents in Iraq.[10]

Meanwhile, the U.S. and Pakistani forces have still not managed to achieve anything decisive in the border area between Afghanistan and its next-door neighbor. In 2004, the offensive in Waziristan of a Pakistani force of 11,000, previously announced as decisive, ended in a humiliating truce with the tribal chiefs, while some 400 to 600 Al Qaeda militants were reportedly still hiding in the border area.[11] And some 18,000 Islamist militants are said to be still active in more than sixty countries.[12]

But the gloomiest predictions were not realized. The "Arab

street" did not rise up, and Iraq's unity was preserved. It would be dishonest to condemn the U.S. policy for the reason that it is centered only on force: there is in the United States a real effort to understand the Islamic-Arab world and an effort of introspection about the sources of anti-U.S. hatred, as well as an acute consciousness of the limits of military force. Moreover, Washington had undertaken through an ambitious "U.S.–Middle East Partnership Initiative" to support efforts for political and social reform in the area.[13] The United States wished next to go to a higher speed with an initiative for political reform in the Broader Middle East, whose scope was somewhat weakened after a discussion in the framework of the G8. (It henceforth stresses partnership with the region's countries.)

True, the struggle against terrorism serves as a justification for blameworthy practices affecting freedom (such as the treatment of the Guantánamo prisoners or that of foreigners rightly or wrongly suspected of links to terrorism). True, the Pentagon acts like an imperial power in the Middle East (for example, in the conditions for awarding reconstruction contracts in Iraq). True, the theme of the "war against dictatorships" would be more credible if the United States refrained from making tactical alliances with authoritarian regimes. And the scorn of much of the U.S. ruling class for the UN, as well as the hubris that motivates its hostility to some of the foundations of the international system, are utterly condemnable.

All the same, the United States deserves praise for asking real questions. Why should the international system continue working on the basis of rules enacted by the winners of a conflict more than sixty years ago? How can the mechanisms for collective security and the rules of international law take account of the actors and threats that didn't exist when these instruments were forged? How can the strategy of deterrence go on being applied when it comes to fanatical leaders or stateless actors? Why maintain regimes of arms control that have the goal of codifying a vanished bipolar balance? And what can be done when the instruments of nonproliferation reach their limits in the face of the determination of some countries to acquire these instruments of power? Criticism of U.S. policy is not always persuasive, for example the "double standards" indictment: must we sacrifice the fate of populations in the name of intellectual rigor, and prefer justice for no one to justice for a few?

In fact, the real problems rest less in the motives and goals of U.S. strategy than in the consequences of its implementation and in the uncertainty of the nature of its long-term objectives. The strategy followed by the United States generates its own dynamics of escalation, fueled by the radicalization of the Arab and Muslim worlds. It produces perverse effects, with a recrudescence of terrorism and proliferation. Finally, it is directed at an enemy that will never be totally conquered, but with which no compromise is possible. For all these reasons, the combat started by the United States increasingly takes on the character of what could be called a "war without end."

THE DYNAMICS OF ESCALATION

It isn't necessary to be a disciple of Clausewitz or a follower of the "Powell doctrine" to realize that in war the lack of a clear-cut goal and exit strategy lead to trouble, and that, once begun, conflicts bear within themselves their own dynamics of escalation. At present, because it has unleashed powerful political, ideological, and religious forces, the United States is no longer in control of the course of this war.

The undesirable political effects are piling up. Washington has shown an extraordinary capacity for losing its partners as fast as they had been won to the U.S. cause after September 11, causing the withdrawal of its best allies (Germany and Turkey) and its great neighbors (Canada and Mexico). Rejection of U.S. policies has become a winning electoral argument. The majority of the Turkish population is now opposed to the war against terrorism.[14] On September 12, 2001, The French newspaper *Le Monde* proclaimed, "We are all Americans"; on May 14, 2004, after the revelations about torture in Iraq, the paper ran the headline, "All Non-Americans?" In Europe the United States' image has reached unprecedented lows.[15] Never has the United States been so powerful militarily, but never has it been so lacking in political credibility.[16] The impressive number of allies in the war in Iraq boasted by the White House concealed the fact that considerably fewer countries were in the 2003 coalition than in that of 1991.[17] China and Russia show signs of resistance and, in the face of the U.S. advance in Asia, seek to advance their own pawns. (For the first time since the end of the Cold War, Moscow has opened new bases abroad, one in Tajikstan and one in Kyrgyzstan, a few miles from a U.S. base; in Cuba, Beijing may be on its way to take the place of Russia).

In fact, the United States has taken such an imposing place on the international geopolitical scene that it can no longer take the liberty of withdrawing on pain of creating power vacuums that would immediately be filled by others. A U.S. retreat from central Asia, for example, would now certainly lead to a competition of powers: thus it has been said that "it could be too late to roll back the Bush administration's aggressive policy because now other countries are emulating that policy."[18] The United States' going to war coincided with the revival of nationalism in major states (Russia, India, and China). Some suggest that resistance to U.S. power fueled a dynamic of war that the United States can't control:

> The hawks . . . will continue to push, because if they
> don't push forward, they will fall back. . . . This
> chaotic world situation will now go on for the next
> twenty or thirty years. No one controls it, least of all
> the United States government.[19]

In this context the concept of preventive military action naturally creates emulators. Russia is said to be interested.[20] India
seemed to be tempted to do the same in 2002, during its military
confrontation with Pakistan.[21] Israel applies more than ever a
comparable strategy: strikes on the Syrian territory and assassination of the Hamas leaders. This is true also for potential adversaries of the United States. The Iranian leadership warned in 2004
that Washington did not have the monopoly on preemptive action.[22] And the struggle against terrorism henceforth is the alibi
of choice for all the governments that want to impose a turn of
the screw on their populations. In this situation, respect for human rights rapidly deteriorates.[23] Finally, the logic of imperialism
allows no turning back. Conquest creates new boundaries to be
stabilized—and this in the absence of a real challenger, as with
past empires.[24]

Worse yet, the war against terrorism radicalizes the Arab and
Muslim populations, which promotes a real political confrontation between Islam and the West. Hardly considered sympathetic
to Washington and Tel Aviv in the first place, the Arab population
imputes all the world's ills to the United States and Israel. The majority of Muslims refuse to believe that their coreligionists are responsible for the attacks of September 11, and a significant
number of them are persuaded that those attacks were the product
of a plan to strengthen an alleged U.S.-Zionist yoke on the Middle East.[25] In the region, Saddam Hussein was frequently consid-

ered a great defender of the Palestinian cause and the only Arab leader to really stand up to Israel. Bin Laden's fatwa against the Jews and the Crusaders (1998) condemned Washington for its actions against Iraq, its supposed subservience to Israel, and its occupation of the Arabian peninsula. Consequently, the fatwa decreed the rule to "kill Americans and their allies, whether civilian or military," in order to bring on the liberation of the holy places in Saudi Arabia and Palestine.[26] We can in a certain way understand the seductive power of such a person on Muslim populations, a power reinforced by some statements of the evangelicals and the neoconservatives. Saddam Hussein dreamed of being seen as a new Saladin: the role now being vacant, bin Laden seems not badly placed to claim it.

Anti-American feeling was already shared by a majority of the populations in many Middle Eastern countries, notably in the United States' allies of Saudi Arabia and Kuwait. But the United States now receives more than 80 percent negative opinions in Morocco, the United Arab Emirates, Jordan, and the Palestinian territories, as well as Indonesia and Pakistan. No doubt even more seriously, in certain countries like Egypt, the opposition to the United States is sometimes based as much on the perception of a difference in values as on U.S. policy itself. As for the possibility of a lasting peace in the Middle East, pessimism is gaining ground. The populations of the Muslim countries are expressing a "vote of confidence" in Osama bin Laden and fundamentalism is growing in countries as diverse as Nigeria and Pakistan, as well as Southeast Asia.[27]

Despite efforts of the White House, the coalition led by the United States in Iraq has appeared to be a "WASP coalition."[28] The war has toned down the old rivalry between Arab nationalism and radical Islam and "has accentuated the polarization between a Muslim 'us' and a Western 'them.'"[29] From Iraq to Palestine, yesterday's adversaries are forming alliances against the United States and Israel.[30] The inferiority complex of the Arab countries in the face of Western armies, maintained by six military defeats, has probably not been attenuated by the speed of the Anglo-U.S. offensive on Baghdad.[31] To say nothing of those who saw the operation as the materialization of a promise allegedly made by Abraham to the Jewish people—a land stretching from the Nile to the Euphrates. Finally, in the Arab and Muslim world, the position of the moderates is weakened by the U.S. policy. Conversely, the Iranian conservatives, for example, have probably been strengthened by the inclusion of Tehran in an "axis of evil" in 2002.[32]

Beyond all that, the Muslim world finds it hard to understand how the United States can position itself as a champion of democracy and human rights while it lives apart from the new instruments of international humanitarian law (the UN Convention of the Rights of Children, the Ottawa Treaty on the prohibition of antipersonnel landmines, the Rome treaty creating the International Court of Justice).[33] The U.S. argument that the United States intervened militarily many times over in order to help Muslim populations, from Bosnia to Afghanistan, is not seen as persuasive. And the argument that Saddam Hussein's torture chambers are henceforth closed was neutralized by the revelations in the spring of 2004 of the mistreatment and torture inflicted on Iraqi prisoners by American guards. Conversely, the alliance with Israel and Russia, the fate of the prisoners of the "war against terror," and the treatment of immigrants from Muslim countries strengthen the view that Americans see Islam as evil.

The claim that the deep causes of terrorism are to be found in U.S. policy is not convincing. If sociocultural rootlessness and the inability of Middle Eastern governments to assure their populations a minimum standard of well-being facilitate recruiting volunteers, Islamist terrorism has origins that are far more complex than poverty and underdevelopment or the lack of a settlement of the Palestinian question.[34] (It isn't the poorest countries in the world that produce terrorism, and bin Laden did not care about Palestine until recently.) Likewise, there is no possible comparison between the collateral damage produced by U.S. bombers and the deliberate destruction of civilian populations undertaken by Al Qaeda. And if the events of 1979 (the Iranian revolution, the invasion of Afghanistan) led the United States to further the emergence of an armed Sunni resistance, one cannot forget that the radicalization of Saudi Islam had begun six years earlier. It is indeed in response to the attempted arson of the Grand Mosque of Mecca in 1969 that the Saudi kingdom had initiated its policy of developing Islamic resistance to the West and to Israel.[35]

However, the fact remains that in allying itself during the cold war with the most authoritarian regimes of the Arab and Muslim world, the United States nourished considerable resentment whose full extent it began to understand only just after September 11 and which served as fuel for the explosion of passionate opinions after the attacks. From this viewpoint, America has perhaps fallen into a trap. Like Japan in 1941 and Iraq in 1990, Al Qaeda seems to have underestimated the United States' ability to react against aggression. Wrongly, its leaders had used the precedents of Beirut and Mogadishu to conclude that the United States was weak. Encouraged by the Soviet pullout from Afghanistan and Israel's withdrawal from southern Lebanon, perceived as its own successes, the Islamist movement no doubt believed that the time had come to attack the principal enemy.

But if, conversely, Osama bin Laden's scheme was that the unleashing of military power born of September 11 would turn the Muslim world against the United States, then we can say that this scheme was not necessarily erroneous. (The assassination of Commander Massood forty-eight hours before the attacks in New

York and Washington, destined to weaken the Northern Alliance, shows that bin Laden knew perfectly well that it was necessary to expect a U.S. counterattack against Afghanistan.) Furthermore, the United States itself is locked up in Iraq in what could be called the twofold trap of "Afghanization" and "Palestinization," making the country, for a long time, a focal point for both the anti-imperialistic cause and the Islamist cause.

THE COLLISION OF FUNDAMENTALISMS

The tensions are all the more liable to grow as the Muslim world sees, on the U.S. side, the figure of the adversary become more and more confused with that of Islam. Bernard Lewis, one of the Middle East experts most listened to in Washington, wrote in the 1990s that a clash with radical Islam was inevitable.[36] Some years later, Samuel Huntington, in a much-debated passage of what was to become his most famous book, didn't hesitate to say

> The underlying problem for the West is not Islamic fundamentalism. It is Islam, a different civilization whose people are convinced of the superiority of their culture and are obsessed with the inferiority of their power.

He went on to suggest that the "bloody" character of Islam-dominant regions could be explained by the propensity of the Muslim states to violence, as much outside as inside their borders.[37]

Now, what was a controversial idea in the mid-1990s had become in the early 2000s a matter of a growing consensus in circles close to the administration. Influential conservative ideologists such as William Buckley, Eliot Cohen, Charles Krauthammer, and

Norman Podhoretz began expressing a similar opinion and, with it, their discontent at the moderate line adopted by the president ("Islam is a religion of peace") and the attitude of a state department judged to be pro-Arab. Their reasoning claims to tackle the heart of the problem: they suggest that terrorism is a tactic, not an enemy. In their writings and even if they sometimes deny it, the differentiation between radical Islam, political or militant Islam, and just plain Islam is increasingly tenuous. For Daniel Pipes, terrorism has a political base of 100–150 million people in the Islamic world.[38] The claim of a Muslim exception is supported with arguments: Francis Fukuyama, who sees the Al Qaeda offensive as a rearguard fight ("a desperate backlash against the modern world"), has argued that "Islam is the one major world culture that arguably does have some very basic problems with modernity," which are expressed notably by a rejection of secularism.[39] These ideas are more and more consensual in U.S. political thinking. The Arab world, which is 90 percent Muslim and, it is true, exceptionally undemocratic, is quite particularly pilloried by analysts such as Fouad Ajami or Laurent Murawiec, who speak of an "Arab malady." Others unhesitatingly suggest that the Islamic world is responsible for generating "the collapse of the well-ordered liberal system."[40]

All this is not false, and some of these claims have moreover been validated by UN reports. The problem is that their radical nature and their increasingly strong public expression tend to fuel the resentment of the local populations and elites in the Arab world.

But these analysts are far surpassed on their right by the religious extremists. Robert Morey advocates a "new crusade" and recommends that the next attack against the United States be immediately followed by the destruction of cities sacred to Islam.[41]

Franklin Graham describes Islam as a "very evil and wicked religion."[42] He suggests that the eternal combat between Islam and Christianity will come to an end only at the return of Christ.[43] Mohammed is publicly called a "terrorist" (Jerry Falwell), a "sex deviant" (Jimmy Swaggart), and a "demon-possessed pedophile" (Jerry Vines).[44] Pat Robertson suggests that Muslims are "worse than the Nazis."[45] The moderate evangelicals can only lament, following the example of Richard Cizik, the vice-president of the NAE (National Association of Evangelicals), that Islam "has become the modern equivalent of the Evil Empire."[46]

The evangelical crusade against Islam is organized around two poles: religious proselytism on the ground in order to convert Muslims; and political mobilization in the United States, on the theme of persecution of Christians.[47] Their organizations, which operate sometimes in the guise of humanitarian missions, like Franklin Graham's Samaritan's Purse, now enjoy quite remarkable financial and logistical power. The Campus Crusade for Christ International claims to count on 225,000 volunteers in 190 countries. Some are devoted to the evangelization of the Muslim world, like Frontiers, which has sent some eight hundred missionaries to forty countries. Their target group is what they call the "10/40 window," that is, the areas of the world situated between ten and forty degrees north latitude.

Among political leaders, the talk is more measured: Tom DeLay is content to declare that "Judea-Samaria" belongs to Israel, and Dick Armey to wish for the Palestinians' departure from the territories.[48] The problem is that this rhetoric is not isolated. Some reputed analysts, such as Fred Iklé, blandly suggest using nuclear weapons to destroy Mecca and Medina in the event of a new major terrorist attack on U.S. soil.[49] General Boykin, a high official in the struggle against terrorism, likens Islam to a form of idolatry, and declares that the United States is "a Christian nation" that is fighting "a guy named Satan," and is only feebly reprimanded by the Bush administration.[50] The blistering hate-filled attacks on Islam by the Italian journalist Oriana Fallacci are bestsellers in the West. Consequently, there is no reason to be surprised that more and more Muslims liken the U.S. strategy to a new crusade.[51] And when the United States, the United Kingdom, and Israel come together side by side in the Middle East, it isn't surprising that anti-imperialist rhetoric links up with anti-Semitic themes of the early twentieth century, and that "Christian Zionism" is likened to a "Zionist crusade."[52]

This talk produces political effects that are all the stronger as they are immediately accessible to the populations concerned, by television, satellite, and the Internet, and often without an intermediary (which would make it possible, for example, to differentiate the discourse of the U.S. administration from that of the more raging ideologists). The abusive words of Jerry Falwell have thus caused riots as far away as India.[53] The spectacular growth of evangelism in the world makes one fear an increase in Islamic fears of recolonization, and a multiplication of local tensions and confrontations.[54]

Encouraged by the rise of anti-Islamic feeling in the West, certain Muslim leaders are taking their turn to throw oil on the fire with the at least tacit approval of their peers: in 2003 the president of the Organization of the Islamic Conference delivered one of the most anti-Semitic speeches in recent years and identified the Jews as the principal adversary without being in any way repudiated by the heads of state and government of the so-called moderate Muslim countries.[55]

America claims it is defending "civilization" against "chaos." But it is hard to avoid acknowledging that the current dynamics lend weight, in the end, to the claim of a conflict of civilizations, as had been predicted by Lewis or Huntington. The latter had suggested that Islam and Christianity were by nature destined to be opposed by virtue of their radical differences but also their common features: a propensity to proselytism, identical claims of universality, a teleological vision of history.[56] The attack in Madrid (March 2004) made Europe aware that the Continent was also a target. Samuel Huntington didn't hesitate to say, "just as [bin Laden] sought to rally Muslims by declaring war on the West, he gave back to the West its sense of common identity in defending itself."[57] Pakistani president Musharraf has warned of a new "Iron Curtain" being drawn between Islam and the West. Even Henry Kissinger, usually very far removed from neoconservatism, seems to be resigned to the confrontation.[58]

The fathers of modern fighting Islam, like the Pakistani Abul A'la Al-Mawdudi and the Egyptian Sayyid Qutb, in the twentieth century, had themselves considered that this confrontation was necessary, for the Muslim religion and civilization were in danger of being destroyed by the West. Now between those who judge that Islam is the problem and those who judge that Islam is the solution, the conflict cannot be subject to compromise.

If not a clash of civilizations, we can at least speak of a collision of fundamentalisms, in a strange confrontation of premodern cultures. Didn't we see by the invasion of Iraq an opposition between U.S. missionaries and religious Shi'ites, representing two cultures that could be said to have identical motivations?[59] There are of course substantial differences between the Protestant and the Muslim fundamentalist movements: militant evangelism does not repress women and does not produce large-scale political violence. But the impression of mirror-imaging is no less real, and there are numerous similarities: rejection of the theory of evolution, distrust of the idea of progress, the pursuit of salvation through a return to the ancients, proselytism in the guise of charitable organizations, the use of modern media (there are now "telekoranists"), a culture of paranoia and conspiracy, and a fear of invasion.[60] The two camps have identical agendas in many respects, including revenge of tradition over modernity, which is expressed on both sides by the unleashing of a violence previously repressed by political and social regulation. As a pithy turn of phrase suggests, all fundamentalisms share "the fear of colonization, of experts, of uncertainty, of foreign influence, of science and sex."[61] On the one hand the madrasa of Binori Town (Karachi), on the other, the Dallas Theological Seminary (Texas), each with its version of the coming Armageddon.[62]

This mirror-imaging effect goes beyond the religious dimension. The conservatives on both sides meet up in loathing the moral corruption of the West and in celebrating basic virtues. Certain writers suggest that Saudi Arabia and the American South have in common the brutal power of a caste of "nouveaux riches" springing from a traditional society, acquired through the exploitation of oil resources with the help of imported manpower.[63] Others judge that "the function of fear in politics is something that Americans share with the Arabs: neither one has really known Hobbesian castration—that is to say, submission of the citizen's savage pride to the sovereignty of the state" thus suggesting that the violence now unleashed was not latent and repressed, but consubstantial to the contemporary political cultures of the two worlds.[64] The juxtaposition of barbaric images—torture of Iraqis, throat-slitting and beheading of Americans—intensifies the sense of sacrificial violence released on both sides. Some U.S. analysts are ready to suggest that a source of the behavior of Americans in Iraq is to be sought in the attitude of the neoconservatives toward violence (see chapter 1).[65] To George Bush's "axis of evil," Osama bin Laden replied "chain of Evil."[66]

At any event, it indeed seems that this "mimetic rivalry on a planetary scale" plays a part in the escalation now occurring.[67] The dialectic of mutual fears of the Other can only encourage a rise to extremes.[68]

BACKLASH:
A NEW OUTBREAK OF THREATS

The implementation of the U.S. strategy in fact tends to favor, rather than reduce, the development of the principal threats to which it is addressed: terrorism and proliferation.

Already, the operations in Afghanistan and Iraq have fueled religious fundamentalism and anti-Americanism, and spurred certain extremist groups, as attested by the succession of attacks from Morocco to Indonesia that have taken place since the conquest of Baghdad.[69] The kick into the Afghan anthill by Operation Enduring Freedom also contributed to the growth of the acts of terrorism against the Indian presence in Kashmir and for several months led the two neighbors to the brink of war. Despite the reassuring statements of the State Department, the number of significant acts of international terrorism is rising (124 in 2001, 169 in 2003).[70] The Al Qaeda organization averaged an attack every two years before September 11; the figure in 2004 was one every three months.[71] This wave has now reached the shores of Europe, as shown by the operations in Turkey (December 2003) and Spain (March 2004). The campaign conducted by the United States has strengthened the Islamists' sense of being totally at war against the rest of the world.[72] The movements supporting terrorism are gaining popularity in the Palestinian territories, all the more so as Israeli policy has been radicalized under Ariel Sharon's government. The U.S. operations have contributed to the awakening of Islamist separatist movements in Thailand.[73]

Iraq has become what Afghanistan once was: the privileged theater of jihad against the West, forcing the United States to maintain some 138,000 military personnel there. In a certain way, the intervention in Iraq constituted a new stage in the process of "Israelizing" U.S. policy. Washington maintains an occupation force there for an indefinite duration, while facing up to a constant harassment on the part of forces that are sometimes a form of national resistance, but most of the time are pure and simple terrorism. Moreover, the intervention could indeed have created the very threat that the United States aimed at countering: a collapsed state, scattered biological and nuclear know-how, and the presence of Al Qaeda in Iraqi territory. Some one thousand foreign Islamist militants were thought to be present there in the spring of 2004.[74] Their popularity could grow if the local populations become exasperated with the frequent incompetence or brutality of American soldiers.

This negative dynamic is also at work in the proliferation of weapons of mass destruction. Since the end of the cold war, the former protégés of the two superpowers have been searching for new guarantees of security. The first Gulf War was a real wake-up call: revealing the gap between Western military power and that of the developing countries, it led many of those countries to the conclusion summarized at the time by the Indian chief of staff: one doesn't fight against the United States without nuclear weapons. Now this "Gulf War effect" has since become considerably more pronounced. The U.S. policy creates a sense of insecurity among the leaders of regimes that are opposed, for good or bad reasons, to the power of the United States, and encourages them to speed up their nuclear programs to protect their regimes.

North Korea should perhaps have been taken seriously when it claimed that its nuclear program was justified by Mr. Bush's policy: even paranoiacs can have enemies and being referred to as a member of an axis of evil by a president who declares moreover to "loathe" Kim Jong Il could only bolster North Korea's determination. The country's officials maintain that they are developing nuclear weapons: "to deter an American preemptive attack. . . . We don't want to suffer the fate of Iraq."[75] Iran, whose nuclear program is much more extensive than its energy needs alone require, is probably thinking in similar terms in view of the deployment of U.S. military power in its vicinity. Despite the agreement reached in November 2004, it is questionable whether Tehran has given up this option for good, and Iran would be able to bring it to a successful conclusion within a few years in the absence of intrusive international inspections. Its perception of the regional threat will weigh heavily in its possible decision to go as far as making the nuclear bomb. Saudi Arabia, which fears being abandoned by the United States and observes the rapid progress of the Iranian program, also wonders whether it should seek nuclear power. Riyadh has long maintained a special relationship with Islamabad; Abdul Qadeer Khan, the father of the Pakistani bomb, regularly gave lectures in Saudi Arabia; and the Saudi authorities several times visited Pakistan's nuclear installations in Kahuta. It seems that the nuclear option from now on is a matter of serious thought within the country's ruling circles.

Even Brazil, which in the 1990s had become one of the champions of nuclear disarmament, has shown a new interest in nuclear technology. The political color of the current leadership, with its talk of independence and great power status, reminds us of the extent to which proliferation now depends first on the positioning of nations with regard to what they see as U.S. hegemony.

Finally, the will of the United States to remove any country's ability to blackmail Washington with the help of ballistic missiles now leads to the U.S. deployment of systems to intercept such missiles; the countries that have already massively invested in this area will probably seek to get around this obstacle, including, if need be, increasing the number of their weapons. Moreover, within the framework of U.S. strategy that now upholds preemption, this deployment is henceforth seen as an offensive tool sheltering U.S. territory from military reprisals and thus leaving hands free in Washington to conduct operations against any country judged an enemy. It is thus conducive to furthering the choice of the preemptive option by other powers.

A CONFLICT WITHOUT A WAY OUT

Finally, the very nature of the adversary has placed the bar extremely high.

It is hard to see how it would be possible to completely eradicate a structure that is moving, fluid, and elusive. Al Qaeda is not a traditional terrorist organization: it works as a holding company, providing logistical and financial assistance to franchisees. Such a living organism develops: its functioning adapts to attacks against it. It has sometimes been rightly described as "a complex adaptive system."[76] Chased out of Afghanistan and Pakistan, its militants have found refuge elsewhere, especially in central Asia and the Caucasus.[77] The nebula consists today of a set of regional networks, each operating more or less independent of the other.[78] For many analysts such as U.S. expert Bruce Hoffman, it is now more of an ideology than an organization.[79] Thus, according to another analyst, it is able to fulfill its vanguard mission.[80] At best it can be contained, not eradicated. With all the more reason, the international terrorist threat on the whole, nourished by the vulnerability of modern societies, cannot be totally defeated. In a certain way, the United States has entrapped itself in speaking from the beginning of a "war": as the British historian Michael Howard notes, this creates an expectation for decisive military action.[81] And, as a linguist aptly noted in 2004, the gradual shift in the Bush administration's rhetoric from "war against terrorism" to "global war on terror" has changed the outlook:

> Like wars on ignorance and crime, a "war on terror" suggests an enduring state of struggle—a "never-ending fight against terror and its relentless on-slaughts," as Albert Camus put it in *The Plague,* his 1947 allegory of the rise and fall of Fascism.[82]

The nature of the combat undertaken by the Islamist funda-mentalists does not allow the prospect of negotiation, compro-mise, or coexistence. The reconstruction of the *Umma* (the community of believers) and the restoration of the caliphate are only tactical objectives: the war should be extended to wherever the sharia is not applied. Therefore, nearly all the world can be-come the *Dar al Harb,* a war zone. Because of the ways it oper-ates, but also because of its goals, the fundamentalist project is in a sense a modern one, a combat with a universal calling led by a revolutionary vanguard: it is not utterly senseless to put it in the same category as Nazism and communism.[83] Taken at face value, the texts and declarations attributed to Al Qaeda have the appear-ance of a rational policy.[84] Beginning in 1996, bin Laden de-manded the withdrawal of U.S. forces from Saudi Arabia and the overthrow of the Saudi regime, and took the view that the attacks committed by Al Qaeda were equivalent to messages that the United States should listen to.[85] After the attacks of 2001 he de-clared that "neither the United States nor he who lives in the United States will enjoy security before we can see it as a reality in Palestine and before all the infidel armies leave the land of

Muhammad"; and, right before the 2004 elections, he said that he sought to "deter" the United States.[86]

However, the U.S. departure from the Arab peninsula and the creation of a sovereign Palestinian state will probably not be sufficient to satisfy Al Qaeda. Its combat against "apostate" regimes is equally important. For Ayman al-Zawahiri, number two in the organization, the land of Islam extends from "Eastern Turkistan to Andalusia."[87] Now, by definition, the reconstitution of the *Umma* on the ruins of some forty member states and the destruction of Israel as a Jewish state cannot be negotiated. Between those who believe that Islam is the problem and seek to stem terrorism and dictatorship, and those who believe that Islam is the solution and seek to stem Western influence, there can only be total war.

The combat has all the fewer possible outcomes as the leaders of Al Qaeda seem as motivated by religion as by a thirst for revenge, a death wish, and a desire for power. Philosopher Lee Harris was not wrong to suggest in this connection that the label "war" hinders us from seeing the true nature of the combat undertaken by the Islamists, which cannot be reduced to a Clausewitzian schema in which force is the means to attain well-defined political objectives.[88]

"Why is it acceptable for us to live with fear, murder, destruction . . . , but peace, security, and happiness should be for you? . . . Now is the time to become equals. Just like you kill us, we will kill you."[89] The goal was even reduced to numbers by Suleiman Abu Gheith, spokesman for the organization: "We have not reached parity with them. We have the right to kill four million Americans—two million of them children."[90] In other words, a few more million dead and we can be even.

Thus, it is not illegitimate to speak of nihilism. For if we can debate the question of whether an Islamist theocracy is totalitarian (a profoundly modern concept), there is in the purifying destruction sought by contemporary Islamist terrorism a dimension that indeed recalls the nihilisms of the twentieth century. However, the total war sought by Al Qaeda does not have a lot in common with the "limited war" of the Russian nihilists.[91] As the philosopher André Glucksmann suggests, Al Qaeda's nihilism corresponds to a restrictive definition of the term, that of a cultivated ignorance of Evil.[92] Because it seeks not total destruction but the destruction of modern civilization and notably that of the Anglo-Saxon West, it is a limited or imperfect nihilism that brings to mind the German nihilism of the twentieth century as analyzed by Leo Strauss.[93] So in a certain sense we can say that the Straussians found their nemesis with Al Qaeda. Had not the Muslim extremists been objective allies of Nazism?

Al Qaeda aims to turn the arms of the United States and Israel against them and thus to establish a "balance of terror."[94] This line of argument is not necessarily insincere. When speaking of these targets, bin Laden says that they are countries that have made the Islamic world suffer.[95] When speaking of means, he specifically refers to Western military history (particularly bombardments during the Second World War) which in truth has had its share of barbaric acts. Despite all that, the argument is not acceptable, for combat today is fundamentally asymmetric. For the West, it is limited by law and culture (neither the deliberate bombardment of civilian populations, nor the offensive use of weapons of mass destruction are tolerable), whereas for Al Qaeda, which justifies its actions by a highly debatable reading of the Koran, there are no limits.

The opposition between those who try to limit the losses and those who try to maximize them can only be absolute. Accordingly,

it is pointless to ask if an organization has a political agenda or only
in fact seeks to destroy. For in the first case, its objectives are not negotiable and in the second, its methods are not negotiable.

A "THIRTY-YEAR WAR"?

The definition of the enemy is getting fuzzier and fuzzier. Is it Islamist terrorism, radical Islam, political Islam? It's becoming hard
to say, and the result of the war is all the more unpredictable as a
result. Is it dictatorship? Is it "chaos"? Is it "evil"? Will the United
States enter into a sort of permanent state of war, similar to, but
on a worldwide scale, the Israeli-Palestinian conflict? Unlike the
Near East conflict, however, the war that began with the attacks
of 2001 cannot be the object of some political solution or some
negotiation.[96] This is the perspective accepted by those of the
U.S. neoconservatives who think, like Michael Ledeen, that
"peace is abnormal," and that "the struggle against evil is going to
go on forever."[97] In 2004 the director of the CIA told the Senate
that the threat will exist "for the foreseeable future, with or without Al Qaeda in the picture."[98] True, this lack of clarity in the
identification of its adversary does give the United States the possibility to announce the end of operations whenever they wish, as
Mr. Bush asserted a few days after the attacks; but only a few
weeks later he said that "So long as anybody's terrorizing established governments, there needs to be a war."[99] This logic, com-
bined with the possibility of conducting military operations called
preemptive but which are, in fact, preventive, leads, as Pierre
Hassner has said, to a permanent state of war whose end can only
be, in theory, "total and . . . totally uncontrolled control" of the
planet by the United States.[100]

Without going that far, the Bush administration and the intellectuals close to it don't hesitate to speak of an effort lasting a

"generation."[101] Vice-Admiral Eric T. Olson, the number two person in the U.S. special forces, declared, "The Americans in high school today are likely the ones who will see this through to the finish."[102]

Thus, it isn't absurd to conjure up, as did Lord Weidenfeld (a figure in the British literary world), a new "war of thirty years."[103] Likewise, James Woolsey did not hesitate to say that the war against terrorism will last for "decades."[104] The image of a fourth world war is not utterly unfounded when we recall that the cold war, in the broadest acceptance of the term, lasted seventy years.

But this comparison with the cold war has its limits. Al Qaeda struck at the heart of America, which the Soviet Union never did. Deterrence is not possible when confronting an enemy without territory, which "hates life itself and worships death." Peaceful co-existence is not an option when faced with an enemy that seeks total destruction. Accordingly, Paul Wolfowitz has suggested, like numerous U.S. analysts, that the combat will last longer than the cold war and will be more difficult than the Second World War.[105]

Hence the pessimistic quote of Dick Cheney that serves as an epigraph to this essay. And as we can trace the beginnings of the cold war to 1917, perhaps one day we will find the beginnings of the "war against terrorism" in the Arab-Israel conflict of 1967, which encouraged the radicalization of the Islamic world, the rise of evangelical views, and the break of U.S. intellectual Jews with the Democratic Party. Osama bin Laden, for his part, substantiated the thesis of this work, in declaring in January 2004 that "The struggle between us and them . . . began centuries ago, and will continue until judgment day."[106]

In any event, the dynamics triggered at the end of 2001 engaged the United States in a very long-term combat. The pursuit of the war is not the subject of a debate in Washington. Neoconservative Tod Lindberg is no doubt correct when he says that

"September 11 transformed American strategic thinking for a generation."[107] Democrats henceforth highlight the imperative of military power and the necessity for the United States "to protect its interests, advance its values, and maintain global order."[108] The philosophy and the vocabulary of the war against terrorism have made their way into the thinking of the entire U.S. establishment. Liberal intellectuals are up in arms against what they consider to be a new totalitarianism.[109] A part of the American left has absorbed certain essential elements of neoconservative doctrine, in particular the moral superiority of America.[110] The theme of "Islamo-fascism" has been taken up by some of the best-known Democratic foreign policy experts; true, certain Democratic figures, such as Richard Holbrooke or Joseph Lieberman, seem sometimes closer to the neoconservatives than to their family of origin. In discussing the foreign policy recommendations of Zbigniew Brzezinski—who is quite far from the neoconservative movement—commentator William Pfaff speaks of "Bush policy given a human face."[111] Democrats do not at all repudiate unilateral military action to defend the security of the United States.[112] During the 2004 presidential campaign, John Kerry spoke of the risk of an attack with weapons of mass destruction as the worst threat that could weigh on the United States and seeks to increase the size of the U.S. military force on duty. He went after Saudi Wahhabism with particular vigor, and foresees in the Islamist threat "a clash of civilization against chaos."[113] Most important, he adopted the Bush concept of a "global war on terror."[114] Whatever their political coloring, the future tenants of the White House will still be presidents at war. Indeed, numerous analysts find the strategy defined under Mr. Bush's first mandate to be, far from a historical exception, a return to the U.S. norm, and that the multilateralism inaugurated by Mr. Roosevelt was a historic exception.[115]

Moreover, the conservative and religious right remains a particularly well-organized movement that guarantees it long-term influence in Congress, whose importance we know in shaping key foreign policy decisions. (The foreign policy followed during Mr. Clinton's second term in office was greatly influenced by Republican views.)

Finally, and this is perhaps the most important, as we have seen, the United States does not control the unfolding of the conflict: it takes two to end a war, and the match is conducted as much in the suburbs of Karachi as in the offices of the Pentagon.

For all these reasons, the U.S. war, like it or not, is at the point of becoming a war without end. The words of historian Charles Beard, who suggested cynically in the era of Soviet-U.S. confrontation that the United States was engaged from the end of the 1940s on in a "perpetual war for a perpetual peace" takes on new meaning today. Leo Strauss, who criticized the illusions in the idea of humanity's march toward a better future, had warned: "Perpetual progress toward perpetual peace means perpetual war."[116]

In retrospect, the grim outlook given by Ralph Peters in 1997 was right on the mark:

> We have entered an age of constant conflict. . . . The have-nots will hate and strive to attack the haves. And we in the United States will continue to be perceived as the ultimate haves. . . . There will be no peace. At any given moment for the rest of our lifetimes, there will be multiple conflicts in mutating forms around the globe. Violent conflict will dominate the headlines, but cultural and economic struggles will be steadier and ultimately more decisive. The de facto role of the U.S. armed forces will be to keep the world safe for

our economy and open to our cultural assault. To those ends, we will do a fair amount of killing. . . . We will not deal with wars of Realpolitik, but with conflicts spawned of collective emotions, sub-state interests, and systemic collapse. Hatred, jealousy, and greed—emotions rather than strategy—will set the terms of the struggle.[117]

5

ALTERNATIVE FUTURES

STILL, THE FUTURE is not written.

September 11 has made us remember that surprise happens in international affairs, and there may very well be other surprises, good or bad, in the coming years. No one knows, for example, how Americans would react to a second attack like September 11, but this time with biological or radioactive agents. If it appeared, for example, that those responsible for a second September 11 were aided by Saudi Arabia, the idea of seizing the oil fields of the kingdom would certainly come up again. But above all the psychological effects of a second major attack would be considerable. General Tommy Franks, who led the wars in Afghanistan and Iraq and is not known to be an extreme-right ideologue, stated at the end of 2003 that in such a situation, the American people could begin to "question our own Constitution and begin to militarize our country. . . . Which, in fact, then begins to potentially unravel the fabric of our Constitution."[1] Without going that far, it is a fact that discussing the reinstitution of the draft is no longer taboo in Washington and some thinkers are worried about what they call the "militarization" of U.S. society.[2]

For what is at stake in this war also concerns the domestic agenda. The fear of another attack remains unchanged in public opinion.[3] The "culture of fear," which has been called a driving force in the functioning of modern U.S. society, is present as never before. It is fed by some of the media (*Fox News*) and political leaders, such as former attorney general John Ashcroft, a committed evangelical and architect of the PATRIOT Act, which restricts liberties in favor of the fight against terrorism.[4] Fundamentalist ideas can be "a formidably effective tool for terrifying a population."[5] The neoconservatives are in general true believers in democracy but since September 11 they take delight in the reaffirmation of traditional values such as patriotism, courage, and self-sacrifice.[6] And the traditional right clearly seems to want to take advantage of the war to take revenge on the liberal left in social and cultural realms.

> One might well ask: "What are we fighting for? The right to watch *Sex and the City* and to legitimate gay weddings?" . . . Can the conditions of personal license and the need for discipline, duty, and loyalty coexist?[7]

What happens next will be determined in large part by the future of two of the planet's most unstable societies, which were given a jolt by the post–September 11 shock wave: Saudi Arabia and Pakistan. On the face of it, these two nations have little in common, except perhaps that they both have very peculiar forms of government (one is run by a family, the other by an army). Saudi Arabia is ruled by one of the most archaic governments on the planet but contains one of the largest petroleum reserves known, as well as the most holy sites of Islam. Pakistan is a major militarized state, with only partial control of its territory, major cities prey to sectarian violence, and nuclear weapons. Still, they have things in common. Both are U.S. allies with major problems linked to rapid population growth, which gives rise to the emergence of an age group without a future unless it be to exacerbate the problem of access to natural resources. Both nations have a major responsibility for the development of Islamist terrorism—each in its own way, but also acting together (the Pakistani madrasas financed by capital from Saudi Arabia). If their cooperation were to extend to a military nuclear program, as is suspected nowadays, the Pakistan–Saudi Arabia pair could become the real axis of evil. Their ruling classes have been targeted explicitly by Al Qaeda, and in the years to come those classes may pay a high price for their strategy of manipulating Islamist movements. Radical forces seem to be gaining ground and, since 2003, we are witness to a growing number of terrorist attacks in the two countries.[8] If either of these countries collapses or explodes, there would be huge repercussions throughout the Arab and Muslim worlds. In that case, the going will get rough. The United States will need to show diplomatic and strategic skill that has not always characterized its actions on Islamic soil. For their part, the Saudi princes and Pakistani military officials will be obliged to engage in an increasingly delicate tightrope act, maneuvering between the U.S. hammer and the Islamist anvil.

The most likely scenario is an enduring tension between Anglo-Saxon society and Arabic and Muslim societies, with the evolution of Saudi Arabia and Pakistan as the central stakes but also with serious peripheral problems (the Korean peninsula). This clash will sometimes have a military dimension and other battles will be fought in the Middle East theater. In some respects, the war against terrorism will resemble the "Barbary wars" fought by the United States in the Middle East in the nineteenth century. But there is no reason to think that the Arab world, or even less the Muslim one, can come together in a federation under a single flag, no more than the United States could persuade the entire West to join its cause. The Arab-Muslim world is even more fragmented than the Western camp. Euro-American tensions during the meetings of the North Atlantic Council look like friendly conversations when compared to those of the Arab League or the Organization of Islamic States, where insults and invectives regularly rain down on the participants. There will be no new battle of Lepanto but rather clashes of identity in which missiles and other arms of nuclear, biological, and chemical warfare are used to challenge the United States and its allies.[9]

But there are other possible scenarios. A return to endemic terrorism in Europe could oblige the West to close ranks and revitalize NATO. A rise in terrorist attacks in Russia, China, and India could give rise to an "Alliance of Major Powers" to confront the nebulous international terrorism, or an "Alliance of Fundamentalisms," Christian, Jewish, and Hindu, against the Islamist enemy.

Or, on the contrary, one can imagine a scenario in which the United States cannot sustain the long-term war effort. The U.S. economy is already structurally in deficit. Washington can only continue to increase its defense budget if the rest of the world is prepared to finance the federal deficit, at the rate of $1.5 billion daily. In this same period, the U.S. has had a quasi-wartime economy, with total defense expenditures close to $500 billion in 2004 (4 percent of the GNP). True, these figures do not approach those during the Second World War, and the size of the U.S. economy today allows it to sustain a war effort much better than it could, for example, during the Vietnam War. But in the absence of another attack on U.S. soil, the American people could demand that their political leaders focus more on unemployment, public health, and education. They seem not to be persuaded by the parallels affirmed between the present war and the Second World War.[10]

The cost of constructing or reconstructing modern states is high. Moreover, there is a disparity in the United States between its military strength and its weakness in nation building. This disparity is all the more striking as Republicans only reluctantly agreed to the latter: initially, Mr. Bush had chosen to break with Clinton politics on this point as on so many others. But the United States learned at great cost on September 11 that a country torn by civil war could be the best breeding ground for radicalism and political violence. So America will have to show determination and patience. Since 1900, only a fourth of U.S.-led experiments in regime change gave birth to democracies within ten years, and a minimum of five years would in any event be necessary for the purpose.[11]

Now, empire building is not in the nature of America. Torn from its very beginnings between interventionism and isolationism, the country that is said to want to police the world is, according to Richard Haas, only a "reluctant sheriff." Mr. Bush has countless times rejected empire building as a U.S. objective, citing the regained sovereignty of Germany and Japan.[12] The application of the term "empire" to the United States has been rejected by both supporters and opponents of his administration.[13] It is true, as one distinguished commentator has said, that something is amiss when applying the term *imperial* to a country that starts reflecting on its exit strategy as soon as it sets foot anywhere.[14] There is no imperialism in the behavior of Americans in the Middle East: instead of taking a place in local life, they withdraw into heavily protected, enclosed spaces. America does not have the equivalent of Roman legions. It cannot occupy a second significant country today in addition to Iraq. (Even if it could, public opinion no doubt would not support government leaders in such a venture.)

The reality is more like a liberal hegemony, or what some have called "empire lite": the United States underinvests substantially compared to what would be necessary for real domination of the imperial kind.[15] Therein lies a major difference from the procedures of past empires, in which conquest was followed by patient building of an administration fully in charge. We are in a different era: the nature of democracies and the cadence of their operation are no doubt incompatible with that sort of undertaking.[16] Perhaps a choice must be made, for "Empires are not built lightly; they are made the hard way or they perish."[17]

Can we conceive of a scenario in which the United States is *defeated*? The armed bands that succeeded in chasing Americans from Mogadishu were, it is said, linked to Al Qaeda: the organization might indeed dream of replaying *Black Hawk Down* on a global scale.[18] In an exceptionally violent account written a decade ago, an author described a scenario in which the United States abandons a military operation in the Middle East under the pressure of public opinion, horrified by bestial torture inflicted upon American female POWs.[19] The proliferation of theaters of operation could weaken the U.S. war machine to the point where a major attack on U.S. forces, or military setbacks, would lead war-weary public opinion to demand that "the boys" be brought back home. Meanwhile, Osama bin Laden and his legions could seize control of the holy sites and provoke the collapse of the Saudi regime, then form a nuclear alliance with an Islamist Pakistan, and might then consider themselves in a position to demand the departure of the Jews from Israel. Another hypothesis not to be rejected out of hand: a tactical alliance between domestic enemies of the federal U.S. government, such as extreme-right militias, sharing certain ideas with the Islamists, and ready to use armed violence (as in the Oklahoma City bombing). Finally, the ultimate nightmare scenario is a nuclear explosion in Washington, an event which would be a form of defeat ("One nuclear explosion in DC and it's game over.").

Such worst-case scenarios have a heuristic value. They allow us to assess the stakes of the current conflicts. But they remain less probable than the displacement of the war on terror by a new bipolar clash—this time with China.

CHINA ON THE HORIZON

It is useful as a conclusion to examine a question that has been overshadowed in strategic analysis since September 11: the evolution of Chinese-U.S. relations. This is the only issue likely one day to take the place of terrorism as a structural element in U.S. strategy.

The complicity between China and the United States in the fight against terrorism has masked the growing friction between the two countries. Yet conflict can only be postponed. The sources of tension in Chinese-U.S. relations are still there. The growing competition for leadership in Asia, and the Chinese will to extend its sovereignty over land and sea areas it considers its own, bring risks of clashes all the greater as Washington has, since the cold war, reinforced its links with southern and eastern Asia for both strategic and economic reasons. Above all, the stakes in Taiwan have grown commensurate with its democratizing and growth in the 1990s. The issue has symbolic value to both sides: for Washington, the defense of democracy and the balance of powers in the region; for Beijing, the unity of the country and the very legitimacy of the Chinese leaders. The Taiwan issue is no doubt the only one that presents a real risk of a Sino-U.S. military clash.

Certainly, Beijing has no intention today of starting the conquest of Taiwan by force. Its priorities are to adapt its economy to the rules of the World Trade Organization, to increase its international recognition by hosting the Olympic Games of 2008, and to catch up militarily with Western nations, particularly by investing in nuclear energy, ballistic missiles, space exploration, and the information war. All observers have praised its positive role in managing the crisis with North Korea. But despite all that, the risks of adventurism are no less real, as an outlet for internal difficulties, or as a reaction to a declaration of independence of the rebel island. As does Russia, China now sees the U.S. armed forces deployed all around its territories. For certain observers, "the United States is needed as an adversary to shore up the legitimacy of the Communist party state."[20] Viewed from the West, the decision to enter into a war over Taiwan would not be rational. But the same might be said of numerous past conflicts: must we remind ourselves that on the eve of the First World War Norman Angell estimated in *The Great Illusion* (1910) that economic interdependence among the European powers would henceforth block all wars among them?

On the U.S. side, the growing trade deficit with the People's Republic—which, to the detriment of U.S. industry, now produces a large part of the manufactured goods consumed by the United States—could make the theme of the Chinese menace increasingly popular. The U.S. deficit vis-à-vis China has grown rapidly: $103 billion in 2002, and $124 billion in 2003. It represents nearly a fourth (23 percent) of the U.S. trade deficit in manufactured goods. The U.S. commercial relation with China is the most imbalanced of any that it has. At the same time, Beijing held in 2004 some $120 billion in U.S. treasury bonds.[21]

Finally, China has climbed in recent years to the rank of second largest petroleum consumer in the world. It presently imports more than 50 percent of its needs, and around 2030 should match the U.S. volume of imports today (10 million barrels daily). China's access to natural resources in its regional environment and in the areas it considers its own, but also in the Middle East, could well lead it to clash with the United States, which is also in search of greater access to diverse sources of energy.[22]

Congress has required the Pentagon to produce an annual report on Chinese military power, which increasingly resembles Soviet military power during the cold war, and neoconservatives have always been opposed to any accommodation with Beijing.[23] Here again, a negative dynamic could unfortunately be at work, so great are the mistrust and ignorance on both sides. Faced with Republican activism, the Clinton administration was not wrong to suggest starting in 1995, in the words of Joseph Nye of the Pentagon, that "to cast China as an enemy would risk creating a self-fulfilling prophecy."[24] Thus we see at work a dynamic analogous to that described earlier between the United States and the Muslim world: mutual distrust, incomprehension, and blunders that could end by validating extremist theses on both sides.

In the worst nightmare of U.S. strategists there would be a counter-alliance between China and the Muslim countries, which would then have as common enemies the United States and extremist Islamist movements. Beyond its historic linkage with Pakistan, the People's Republic has undertaken, essentially for opportunistic reasons, to draw closer to the nations of central Asia and the Persian Gulf, with which relations are often constructed around a fruitful barter—"arms for oil." Beijing is developing its ties with Riyadh, and China has already displaced the United States as the leading consumer of Saudi oil.[25] (The Gulf is expected to provide three-fourths of Chinese crude imports in the decade starting 2010.) China is also drawing closer to Sudan and has deployed several thousand soldiers there to protect a pipeline.[26] Beijing found itself naturally in the position of defender of developing nations with which it feels an affiliation—once the Soviet Union dissolved and India defected—and China has more than once received encouragement from authoritarian regimes pleased about its opposition to Washington. "We wish China victory," said Colonel Ghaddafi in 1994.[27] Of course, the People's Republic does not want to tangle with the United States and will carefully avoid giving the impression of an anti-American front. For their part, business circles in the United States will continue to lobby in favor of peaceful relations. But if the relations between the two countries ever do deteriorate, the capital patiently invested by Beijing in the Islamic world could then be quite precious.

The American enemies of China, united for some years now in an informal network called the Blue Team, have been lying low since September 11. It is true that several of them are in command positions in the administration or in Congress. But the neoconservatives await other opportunities: for that matter, if one believes Robert Kagan, "the long-term goal [of current U.S. policy] is regime change in Beijing."[28] The theme of the Chinese menace could bring together both those who want to block the emergence of a major rival power, and those who are obsessed by the goal of expanding democracy. Does not the People's Republic represent half of the world's population still living under a dictatorial regime? And then there is its repression of religion in the context of the growing success of Christianity in the country, a supplementary motive for U.S. discontent: China today already represents the second largest evangelical population in the world, just behind the United States.[29]

Above all, U.S. adversaries of China can see the day when, in the confrontation with the People's Republic, the final stage in the war on terror will be transformed into a war against dictatorship—in the final analysis, a necessity to declare the total victory of Western democracy over communism. That is, the true "end of history."

"After Baghdad, Beijing," said some neoconservatives in the spring of 2003, while an influential figure in the Pentagon suggested that "Iraq was just a warm-up for China." The authors of these statements were only half kidding. Despite the difficulties and the failures of the U.S. project for the Middle East, the ideology of combative democratizing is not dead. The importance of neoconservatism in U.S. strategy is cyclical: at the right moment, it is quite possible that it will ally itself again with militant evangelism, this time to confront the last great bastion of revolutionary socialism. But this implies a termination, one way or the other, of the war against terror. For this new battle to begin, the war that commenced on September 2001 must come to an end.

AFTERWORD

AND WHAT ABOUT Europe?

Most Europeans do not feel that they are at war. For sure, Islamist terrorists have struck the Continent, its citizens, and its interests abroad more than once since September 11. European governments have been partners in the war on terror, and the most significant non-U.S. military contributions to operations Enduring Freedom and Iraqi Freedom have come from Europe.* But, on the European side of the Atlantic, there is no feeling of being at war. This, along with the hubris of the Bush administration, helps to explain to a large extent the amount of mistrust that has developed across the Atlantic. The Madrid bombings of March 11, 2004, were not the European equivalent of the New York and Washington attacks. The Atocha train station was neither the World Trade Center nor the Pentagon. Despite the horrendous toll, the number of casualties was a tenth of that on September 11. And the attacks happened in a country that had been the target of terrorism for a long time. Thus the sense of shock in Europe on that morning was very different from what it had been across the Atlantic two and a half years earlier. The following day, the French daily *Libération*'s headline was not "All Spaniards," but a much more restrained "All Madriders."

The thesis of an irreversible transatlantic split is appealing. How can it not be hard to reconcile an America that wants to

---

*The exception here is Australia.

destabilize the Middle East with a Europe that strives for peaceful stability? Europe continues to show a willingness to compromise with authoritarian regimes in the name of peace. And that is getting harder and harder to swallow for a post–September 11 America that believes the status quo is not only morally, but also strategically, untenable.

The celebrations of unity for the sixtieth anniversary of D-Day in June 2004 could not hide the lingering effects of the Iraq crisis. Books, pamphlets, and articles published in the United States now regularly stigmatize not only France, but also Europe as a whole, as a strategic enemy. Meanwhile, polls conducted in Europe rank the United States as a major threat to world peace.

More important, September 11 and Iraq have added to a sense of growing divergences since the end of the cold war. The combination of the disappearance of the Soviet threat and the generational change has led to a growing forgetfulness of the bonds forged in the fight against Nazism and reinforced in the long struggle against communism. In the absence of a peer competitor, the sheer difference of power between the United States and any other country or existing alliance in the world limits the incentives for Washington to seek cooperation or exercise self-restraint. Multilateralism and multipolarity are needed by the weak, not by the strong, and the United Nations was created in a world where differences in respective power did not exist to such an extent that it does today. There are strong societal differences between the United States and Europe. The former is a demographically dynamic power, where religion plays a key role in public life, and where, to some extent, norms on the use of physical violence are less stringent than on the Continent. The latter is an aging land, where secularism is becoming the norm, that has sought to ban the use of force inside its borders. For all their shortcomings, there is some value in Kagan-like generalizations about a Hobbesian America and a Kantian Europe.

But why should we care? After all, why should we try to preserve a relationship that may just have passed its time? The answer is simple. We should care because the history of the past decades has given us many clear examples—from the cold war to the Balkans to the Middle East—of how much transatlantic unity can make a difference in the management of world affairs and the handling of crises. Thus it would be a loss to both sides, and perhaps more broadly to the world. Hopefully, the split appears neither as profound nor as irreversible as it seems.

The transatlantic differences need to be put in perspective. There is still a transatlantic community in economic terms. Over the last decade, the United States has invested ten times more in the Netherlands than in China. And Europe invests more in Texas alone than the United States does in Japan. There is also still a transatlantic community in cultural terms. Despite our differences, a Californian and a German have more in common and better chances to understand each other than, say, a Japanese and a Texan. NATO remains the only standing multinational military alliance in the world, and for all the talk about its lost sense of mission, it has shown a remarkable ability to adapt.

Also, the political divisions among Americans, as well as among Europeans, are often as severe as, say, the French-U.S. rift over Iraq. And other alignments of powers transcend the usual and convenient "Europe vs. America" division. When intervention and military power are discussed, the "Big Three" (the United States, the United Kingdom, and France), which are permanent members of the UN Security Council and official nuclear powers, often have similar reflexes. Also, the war on terror has shown that there is a lot in common among political elites in the three key

English-speaking countries (the United States, the United Kingdom, and Australia).

Most important, there is some chance that cold-warlike unity might be resuscitated. Here we need to ask a disagreeable question: will Islamist terrorism be the new glue that unites the West? When NATO secretary general Willy Claes floated that hypothesis in 1994, it was met with a flurry of horrified responses. Things are obviously different today. It might be too early to claim, as Sam Huntington did in a slightly self-serving way, that Osama bin Laden has given back to the West the sense of common identity that it had lost. For that to happen, my guess is that several Madrid-type attacks, or one New York–type attack, would need to take place on European soil. Nobody should rejoice at such a prospect. But the fact is that at the time of this writing (fall of 2004), this hypothesis had moved from the realm of the improbable to at least that of the possible.

Thus the sad reality is that we may face two unappealing futures, one where terrorism is contained and Atlantic unity dissolves, out of fatigue as well as political and social changes on both sides; and the other where terrorism and radicalization in the Islamic world rejuvenate the idea of the West around the common cause of freedom and democracy. Of course, if one reduces that choice to one between peace and unity, it is then a rather easy one. Unfortunately, reality seldom offers politicians and citizens such easy choices.

At the very least, both sides should recognize two fallacies, one in the neoconservative camp, the other in the neopacifist camp. U.S. neoconservatives are wrong when they argue that the war can be won by the United States alone. Allied intelligence has been and will remain indispensable to win the war, if only because of longstanding European investment in penetrating the Middle East terrorist networks. European political ties with the Arab world can prove valuable to shore up the legitimacy of U.S.-led actions. And the economic power of the European Union could be a key asset for the transformation of the broader Middle East.

European neopacifists are even more wrong when they argue that this is an American war that does not concern us. Al Qaeda and its affiliates explicitly target European countries, whether they participated in the war in Iraq or not. The renewed emphasis on secularism in the European Union will make the Continent an increasingly attractive target. (Already Europeans are prime targets for hostage-taking in Iraq.) Many Islamist militants are Europeans or have been educated and trained in Europe. And a failure of the U.S. project in Iraq would have devastating ripple effects on the whole world, certainly making it even less secure in the long run. Finally, to argue that military action is not the appropriate way to deal with terrorism, as some did after the Madrid bombings, is to misconstrue the nature of the adversary.

My hope is that legitimate transatlantic disagreements will not distract Europeans from seeing the bigger picture. It remains to be proven that this is a civilizational war, but it is certainly an ideological war. And we are immersed in it whether we like it or not. There will be other transatlantic clashes concerning the use of military force, and disputes around the definition of what constitutes "last resort." Differences of perspective about the war will continue to exist between Europeans and Americans, as well as among Americans and among Europeans. But at least, may all sides not confuse themselves about who and what the enemy is.

NOTES

INTRODUCTION: BACK TO HISTORY

1. George W. Bush, "President's Remarks at National Day of Prayer and Remembrance" (September 14, 2001).
2. Cited in Bob Woodward, "CIA Told to Do 'Whatever Necessary' to Kill Bin Laden. Agency and Military Collaborating at 'Unprecedented' Level; Cheney Says War Against Terror 'May Never End,'" *Washington Post*, October 21, 2001.
3. Alexandre de Marenches and David A. Andelman, *The Fourth World War: Diplomacy and Espionage in the Age of Terrorism* (New York: William Morrow, 1992).
4. Ralph Peters, "Constant Conflict," *Parameters*, Summer 1997, 4–14.
5. George F. Will, "The End of Our Holiday from History," *Washington Post*, September 12, 2001.
6. Pierre Hassner, "Fin de l'histoire ou phase d'un cycle?" *Commentaire*, Autumn 1989.
7. Condoleezza Rice quoted in David E. Sanger, "Rice Faults Past Terrorism Policy," *International Herald Tribune*, November 1, 2003.
8. Ivo H. Daalder and James M. Lindsay, *America Unbound: The Bush Revolution in Foreign Policy* (Washington, DC: Brookings Institution Press, 2003), 83.
9. See Condoleezza Rice, "Opening Remarks to Commission on Terrorist Attacks" (Hart Senate Office Building, Washington, DC, April 8, 2004).
10. David Frum, *The Right Man: The Surprise Presidency of George W. Bush* (New York: Random House, 2003), 142.
11. Hendrik Hertzberg and David Remnick, "The Trap," *The New Yorker*, October 1, 2001.
12. Barry R. Posen, "Command of the Commons: The Military Foundation of U.S. Hegemony," *International Security* 28, no. 1, Summer 2003.

1. INTERPRETING THE BUSH REVOLUTION

1. Daalder and Lindsay, *America Unbound*, 75.

2. Richard Armitage, Robert Blackwill, Stephen Hadley, Condoleezza Rice, Richard Perle, Paul Wolfowitz, Dov Zakheim, Robert Zoellick.

3. See for example Charles Krauthammer, "The New Unilateralism," *Washington Post*, June 8, 2001.

4. Frum, *The Right Man*, 66.

5. Douglas Jehl, "CIA slow to move against terror threat," *International Herald Tribune*, April 15, 2004.

6. Ms. Rice did assert that the presidential directive adopted September 4, 2001, (NSPD-9) provided for the "elimination" of Al Qaeda. Rice, "Opening Remarks to Commission on Terrorist Attacks."

7. Paul Wolfowitz quoted in Daalder and Lindsay, *America Unbound*, 81.

8. Benjamin Barber, *Jihad vs. McWorld: How the Planet Is Both Falling Apart and Coming Together and What It Means for Democracy* (New York: Times Books, 1995).

9. Bob Woodward, *Plan of Attack* (New York: Simon and Schuster, 2004), 87.

10. George W. Bush, "A Period of Consequences" (The Citadel, South Carolina, September 23, 1999). See also Condoleezza Rice, "Promoting the National Interest," *Foreign Affairs*, January–February 2000.

11. Daalder and Lindsay, *America Unbound*, 30.

12. This sentence refers to the work by Jean-François Revel, *Ni Marx ni Jésus* (Paris: Robert Laffont, 1970).

13. The PNAC and AEI are located in the same building in the heart of Washington. (Some twenty Bush administration officials came from the AEI.) Other influential conservative think tanks are the Heritage Foundation, the Hoover Institution, the Hudson Institute, the Center for Security Policy, and the discreet Claremont Institute.

14. Several figures in the neoconservative movement were inspired by James Burnham and Max Shachtman, American disciples of Trotsky.

15. The expression "neoconservative" was coined by Michael Harriman and the magazine *Dissent*. Jonah Goldberg, "The Neoconservative Invention," *National Review*, May 20, 2003. Some, like Joshua Muravchik, Richard Perle, Gary Schmitt, and James Woolsey, still consider themselves Democrats. Some historic figures in the movement have a very different profile, such as, notably,

the Catholic William Bennett, secretary of education under Reagan, an ardent partisan of "moral clarity."

16. Ibid.

17. Irving Kristol, "The Neoconservative Persuasion," *Weekly Standard,* August 25, 2003.

18. Wohlstetter inspired in particular Richard Perle, Paul Wolfowitz, Zalmay Khalilzad, William Luti, . . . and even Ahmed Chalabi, the candidate preferred by the Pentagon for the administration of Iraq.

19. He was the thesis adviser for Paul Wolfowitz, whose thesis dealt with the risk of proliferation resulting from the usage of nuclear energy to desalinate seawater in the Middle East.

20. Fred C. Iklé and Albert Wohlstetter, "Discriminate Deterrence: Report of the Commission on Integrated *Long-Term Strategy,*" January 1988. This report sounded the alarm on the emergence of new military powers, such as China, and expressed concern over the complexity of a "multipolar" world. It advocated diversification of American options, supported "discriminative" technologies, allowing the use of force at adequate levels for limited crises, and antimissile defense. It also recommended the diversification of American armed-forces bases.

21. Henry Jackson put his name on a famous amendment written by Richard Perle, making most-favored nation status for the Soviet Union conditional on freedom of emigration.

22. This opposition is well described by Zbigniew Brzezinski in James Mann, *Rise of the Vulcans: The History of Bush's War Cabinet* (New York: Viking Penguin, 2004), 97.

23. Paul Wolfowitz was then at the Pentagon.

24. For Richard Perle, the failure of the international community in Bosnia was a turning point in the awareness of the neoconservatives. Panorama, *The War Party,* BBC-1, May 18, 2003.

25. William Kristol and Robert Kagan, "Toward a Neo-Reaganite Foreign Policy," *Foreign Affairs*, July–August 1996.

26. The letter of January 26, 1998, was cosigned in particular by Messrs. Abrams, Armitage, Bolton, Fukuyama, Kagan, Kristol, Khalilzad, Perle, Rodman, Rumsfeld, Woolsey, Wolfowitz, and Zoellick.

27. John Ehrmann, *The Rise of Neoconservatism: Intellectuals and Foreign Affairs, 1945–1994* (New Haven: Yale University Press, 1995).

28. The founding fathers of this movement saw themselves in the beginning as "neoliberals."

29. Leo Strauss, *The City and Man* (Chicago: University of Chicago Press, 1978), 6. It would be difficult to cite Strauss in order to justify the struggle between civilizations: this author's thinking was in part built around a dialogue of cultures (his reading of Plato was inspired by Eastern philosophers).

30. For a long time Strauss had been considered one of the most powerful intellectual figures for the conservative milieu. See Jacob Weisberg, "The Cult of Leo Strauss: An Obscure Philosopher's Washington Disciples," *Newsweek*, August 3, 1987; and Richard Lacayo, "But Who Has the Power?" *Time*, June 17, 1996.

31. Daniel Tanguay, *Leo Strauss: une biographie intellectuelle* (Paris: Grasset, 2003), 136.

32. Thomas G. West, *What Would Leo Strauss Say about American Foreign Policy?*, Constitution Day Colloquium on Leo Strauss and America, Claremont Institute, September 16, 2003.

33. Seymour Hersch, "Selective Intelligence," *The New Yorker*, May 5, 2003. Here in fact is a concept that comes down to us from classical philosophy: for Socrates, the philosopher should not reveal that he does not believe in God for such beliefs are necessary for respect of the law (and because he himself could be subject to persecution); for Farabi, refraining from challenging religious belief aided in elevating the mind.

34. A good introduction to the influences of Strauss and Wohlstetter is provided by Alain Frachon and Daniel Vernet, "Le stratège et le philosophe," *Le Monde*, April 16, 2003.

35. Strauss, *The City and Man*, 4–5.

36. Allan Bloom, *The Closing of the American Mind* (New York: Simon and Schuster, 1987).

37. It was Leo Strauss who introduced Bloom and Kojève.

38. Kojève nevertheless had a certain pessimism, for the end of history would change human nature. For his part, Bloom regretted the modernity of American culture, which in his view led to nihilism.

39. Fukuyama's article had been considered optimistic by his mentor, who responded that "fascism has a future if not *the* future." Allan Bloom, "The Moment of the Philosophy," *Commentary*, Autumn 1989, 472.

40. ". . . a decisive victory for the forces of freedom—and a single sustainable

model for national success: freedom, democracy and free enterprise." *The National Security Strategy of the United States,* September 2002, introduction.

41. George W. Bush, "A Distinctly American Internationalism" (Ronald Reagan Presidential Library, Simi Valley, CA, November 19, 1999).

42. Richard Cheney, "Remarks by the Vice–President to the World Economic Forum" (Congress Center, Davos, Switzerland, January 24, 2004).

43. Richard Slotkin, *Regeneration through Violence: The Mythology of the American Frontier, 1600–1860* (New York: HarperPerennial, 1996), 36–37, 45.

44. The Southern Baptist Convention was the only major Protestant church to approve the war against Iraq. It includes half of the American Baptist community (sixteen to eighteen million members out of thirty-four to thirty-six million).

45. Estimates vary considerably. Forty-five percent of the adult population (some eighty million people) call themselves "born again" or "evangelical."

46. Franklin Graham was invited to give the benediction at the Republican conventions of 1996 and 2000, and at the inauguration of Mr. Bush, where he was reproached for reference to the "Lord Jesus Christ," breaking with the ecumenical tradition on such an occasion. This didn't prevent his being invited to give the benediction at the Pentagon on Holy Friday, in the middle of the war against Iraq.

47. See the extraordinary popular success of Tim LaHaye's series Left Behind, Bible stories whose eleventh volume, *Armageddon,* came out in 2003, and whose twelfth and last volume, *Glorious Appearing,* appeared in 2004. The books, including the audio and children's versions, had press runs all told of some sixty-two million copies, in addition to products based on the series.

48. His book *The Late Great Planet Earth* (1970) sold some thirty-five million copies.

49. It is personified by the Worldwide Church of God, which is today part of NAE (National Association of Evangelicals) and has rejected its Anglo-Israeli heritage. Attached to the Adventist movement, it has some sixty thousand members.

50. It is thus opposed to certain premillenarian dogmas such as that of "rapture."

51. Representing between fifty thousand and one hundred thousand people, the Christian Identity inspired the bombing in Oklahoma City (1993) attributed to Timothy McVeigh, and performed on the anniversary of the tragedy of Waco (Texas). Eighty-one members of the fundamentalist sect Branch Dravidians died in Waco.

52. Robert Shogan, *Constant Conflict: Politics, Culture, and the Struggle for America's Future* (Boulder, CO: Westview Press, 2004), 249.

53. According to a Harris poll, 68 percent of Americans in 2003 believed in the existence of the devil. A study conducted by the National Opinion Research Center of the University of Chicago in 1991 revealed a great difference with Europe: 45.4 percent of Americans said then that they believed with certainty in the existence of the devil, contrasted with 3.6 percent to 24.8 percent in Europe, depending on the region (an exception was Northern Ireland, 43.1 percent).

54. Paul Weyrich, a strategist of the Christian right, was one of the founders of the Heritage Foundation, a common ground for neoconservatives and traditional conservatives. And Elliott Abrams, an adviser to Mr. Reagan, sought to promote ties between the Christian right and Jewish intellectuals.

55. See the 1992 studies of American strategy conducted by Messrs. Cheney and Wolfowitz, the 1998 makeup of the Congressional Policy Advisory Board (including, among others, Messrs. Cheney, Rumsfeld, Wolfowitz, and Ms. Rice), and in the same era the Rumsfeld/Wolfowitz commission on the proliferation of ballistic missiles.

56. Proposed, respectively, by Democrat Ivo Daalder and Republican Charles Krauthammer.

57. See Jacob Heilbrunn, "Neocon vs. Theocon: The New Faultline on the Right," *New Republic,* December 30, 1996.

58. On this point and the justification of the neoconservatives, see Michael Lind, *Made in Texas: George W. Bush and the Southern Takeover of American Politics* (New York: Basic Books, 2002), 150–51.

59. Ibid., 115. Among the rare "bridges" between these two cultures, one must mention the original case of Marvin Olasky, a Jewish neoconservative converted to Protestant fundamentalism and the inspiration of the "compassionate conservatism" dear to George W. Bush. Olasky's book *The Tragedy of American Compassion* (1992) had already had substantial influence on Newt Gingrich, the majority leader of the House of Representatives in 1994.

60. This is organized by the network of the National Unity Coalition for Israel, which represents two hundred Jewish and Christian organizations, and claims to represent forty million Americans.

61. In April 2002, Mr. Netanyahu shocked everyone by comparing the Palestinians to Mexicans.

62. Lynne Cheney, former director of the National Endowment for the Humanities, is known for her opposition to multiculturalism and her defense of moral clarity in education.

63. Francis Fukuyama, Zalmay Khalilzad, Andrew Marshall, Laurent Murawiec, Donald Rumsfeld, Abram Shulsky, Ashley Tellis, and Albert Wohlstetter, among others, spent some time there in one capacity or another.

64. Until February 2004, Mr. Perle was a member of the Defense Policy Board, which he chaired from 2001 to 2003.

65. In 2002, Jeanne Kirkpatrick expressed the view that Wolfowitz was "still a *leading* Straussian." Quoted in Mann, *Rise of the Vulcans,* 28.

66. George W. Bush, "Remarks by the President to a Special Session of the German Bundestag—President Bush Thanks Germany for Support Against Terror" (May 23, 2002); Bush, "Remarks by the President at 2002 Graduation Exercise of the United States Military Academy" (June 1, 2002).

67. Condoleezza Rice, "Discusses President's National Security Strategy" (Waldorf Astoria Hotel, New York, October 1, 2002).

68. Eliot Cohen, "World War IV," *Wall Street Journal,* November 20, 2001. The neoconservatives imitate their elders, who early on identified the cold war as the "third world war."

69. Full text of message to Iraqis, www.aljazeera.net, October 19, 2003.

70. David Frum and Richard Perle, *An End to Evil: How to Win the War on Terror* (New York: Random House, 2003), 9, 222.

71. George W. Bush, "Statement by the President in His Address to the Nation" (September 11, 2001).

72. Bush, "President's Remarks at National Day of Prayer."

73. Bush, "A Distinctively American Internationalism."

74. Frum, *The Right Man,* 238.

75. Michael Novak, "The Return of Good and Evil," *Wall Street Journal,* February 7, 2002.

76. Bush, "Remarks by the President at the 2002 Graduation Exercise." The expression "moral clarity" is associated with neoconservative William Bennett. However, it was a theme shared by the presidencies of Theodore Roosevelt and Woodrow Wilson (Strobe Talbott, "War in Iraq, Revolution in America," *International Affairs,* October 2003, 795, 1040).

77. See the study *Transatlantic Trends 2003* conducted by the German Marshall Fund of the United States.

78. "To be American, what does that mean? It is to have discovered the secret of

seizing metaphysical privilege from the Jews." Peter Sloterdijk in Alain Finkielkraut and Peter Sloterdijk, *Les Battements du monde* (Paris: Pauvert, 2003), 31.

79. See Ivo H. Daalder and James M. Lindsay, *The Bush Revolution: The Remaking of America's Foreign Policy* (Washington, DC: Brookings Institution Press, 2003), 27.

80. See for example the quote of the Gospel According to Saint John ("And the light shines in the darkness. And the darkness will not overcome it") in George W. Bush, "President's Remarks to the Nation" (Ellis Island, New York, September 11, 2002).

81. Quoted in Slimane Zeghidour, "Les Croisés de l'Apocalypse," *Nouvel Observateur,* February 26–March 3, 2004, 18.

82. David Sanger, "All Pumped Up and Nowhere to Go," *New York Times*, July 9, 2000.

83. Mark Strichez, "Born Again. The ranks of Christian Conservatives Are Not Dwindling," *Weekly Standard*, January 17, 2004.

84. One can mention as moderating forces Ms. Rice and also her two assistants, Stephen Hadley and Robert Blackwill, or Franklin Miller, responsible for defense issues.

85. See Max Boot, "Think Again: Neocons," *Foreign Policy,* January–February 2004; and William J. Bennett, "Thoughts on Iraq and the War on Terrorism," Heritage Lectures, 819, February 3, 2004.

86. See Frum, *The Right Man*; and Bob Woodward, *Bush at War* (New York: Simon and Schuster, 2002).

87. For example, Elliott Abrams, in charge of Near Eastern affairs, or Robert Joseph, in charge of nonproliferation, close to Mr. Cheney.

2. WAGING THE FOURTH WORLD WAR

1. It is also an economic war for the adversary camp: Osama bin Laden took public pleasure in the drop on Wall Street after the September 11 attacks and in the increased American deficit. Full text of message to the Iraqis, www.aljazeera.net.

2. George W. Bush, "Address to a Joint Session of Congress and the American People" (September 20, 2001).

3. Real "international" networks are few. Other than Al Qaida, Jemaah Islamiyah no doubt merits this label, as does the Zarqawi network.

4. Quoted in "Plans for Iraq Attack Began on 9/11," CBSNEWS.com, September 4, 2002.

5. Bush, "Statement by the President in His Address to the Nation" (September 11, 2001).

6. Bush, "Address to a Joint Session of Congress and the American People."

7. The expression "weapons of mass destruction" covers, in the terminology of the UN, nuclear, biological, chemical, and radiologic means. Their launchers, particularly ballistic missiles, are sometimes by extension placed in the same category.

8. Lee Harris, *Civilization and Its Enemies: The Next Stage of History* (New York: Free Press, 2004), 31.

9. George W. Bush, "Remarks Aboard the USS *Abraham Lincoln* Announcing Combat Operations in Iraq" (San Diego, May 1, 2003).

10. The American withdrawal from Lebanon in 1983 seems to have had an influence on the young bin Laden.

11. Norman Podhoretz, "How to Win World War IV" *Commentary,* February 2002; James R. Woolsey, "World War IV" (Restoration Weekend Address, November 16, 2002).

12. See for example George W. Bush, "Address of the President to the Nation" (September 7, 2003).

13. Max Boot, "Iraq War Can Make Up for Earlier U.S. Missteps," *USA Today,* March 25, 2003.

14. The expression "democratic peace" was taken up by Mr. Bush, "State of the Union Address" (United States Capitol, Washington DC, January 20, 2004).

15. Woodrow Wilson, "Address to Congress," *Congressional Record,* April 2, 1917.

16. Cited in Frum, *The Right Man,* 234.

17. Prayer read on the radio by President Roosevelt on June 6, 1944.

18. Bush, "Address to a Joint Session of Congress and the American People."

19. George W. Bush, "Remarks by the President at the Twentieth Anniversary of the National Endowment for Democracy" (November 6, 2003). This site was chosen intentionally by the Bush administration. The National Endowment for Democracy was indeed born of the 1982 address.

20. Rice, "Discusses President's National Security Strategy."

21. John B. Judis, "Trotskyism to Anachronism: The Neoconservative Revolution," *Foreign Affairs,* July–August 1995.

22. Lee Harris, "Our World-Historical Gamble," *Tech Central Station,* March 11, 2003.

23. "An Interview with Historian Andrew Roberts," Aspen Institute Berlin, May 2004.

24. Pierre Hassner, *La Terreur et l'empire. La violence et la paix II* (Paris: Seuil, 2003), 199; Stefan Halper and Jonathan Clarke, *America Alone: The Neo-Conservatives and the Global Order* (Cambridge: Cambridge University Press, 2004), 181.

25. For some years, the countries known to support terrorism directly and repeatedly have been, for the State Department: North Korea, Cuba, Iraq, Iran, Libya, the Sudan, and Syria.

26. India, Israel, and Pakistan are not parties to the Treaty on the Non-Proliferation of Nuclear Weapons. North Korea, Egypt, Iraq, Libya, Syria, and Taiwan, among others, are not signatories to the Chemical Weapons Convention. (Israel has signed but not ratified the Convention.) Israel and the Sudan, among others, are not signatories to the Biological Weapons Convention. (Egypt and Syria have signed but not ratified the Convention.)

27. Daalder and Lindsay, *America Unbound*, 120.

28. Richard Perle, interview in *Le Figaro,* August 28, 2003.

29. See Condoleezza Rice, "Promoting the National Interest," *Foreign Affairs,* January–February 2000.

30. The United States wishes to see "the transformation of the DPRK into a normal state" in the words of the State Department. Marina Malenic, "U.S. Seeks 'Transformation' of North Korea," *Global Security Newswire,* March 15, 2004.

31. Woodward, *Plan of Attack,* 87.

32. Clinton himself resorted to this rhetoric in 1998, speaking of "an unholy axis of terrorists, drug traffickers and organized international criminals." Bill Clinton, "President's Address to the Joint Chiefs of Staff and Pentagon Staff" (February 17, 1998).

33. George W. Bush, "The President's State of the Union Address" (January 29, 2002).

34. George W. Bush, "Remarks by the President at the United States Air Force Academy Graduation Ceremony" (Falcon Stadium, USAF Academy, June 2, 2004).

35. Messrs. Edelman, Khalilzad, Libby, and Wolfowitz, as well as Andrew Marshall and Albert Wohlstetter, participated. The document also raised the question of using preventive military force against a country developing weapons

of mass destruction, and extolled the virtues of ad hoc coalitions. See "Excerpts from the Pentagon's Plan: 'Prevent the Re-Emergence of a Rival,'" *New York Times,* March 8, 1992; and Mann, *Rise of the Vulcans.* The themes of world leadership and American military preeminence intended to prevent any competitors were developed in the later writings of Mr. Khalilzad. See for example, "Strategy and Defense Planning for the Coming Century" in Zalmay M. Khalilzad and David M. Ochmanek, *Strategic Appraisal 1997* (Santa Monica: Rand Corporation, 1997).

36. "At present the United States faces no global rival. America's grand strategy should aim to preserve and extend this advantageous position as far into the future as possible." The document added in a later section that the "transformation" of the armed forces sought would take time "absent some catastrophic and catalyzing event—like a new Pearl Harbor." *Rebuilding America's Defenses: Strategy, Forces, and Resources for a New Century,* PNAC, September 2000.

37. *The National Security Strategy*, introduction.

38. On the imperative to reinforce international cooperation as a means of struggle against terrorism, see for example, George P. Shultz, "An Essential War: Ousting Saddam Was the Only Option," *Wall Street Journal,* March 29, 2003.

39. In 2003, the United States consumed twenty million barrels a day (MMBD), 12.2 of them imported (including 2.1 MMBD from Canada and 1.8 MMBD from Saudi Arabia).

40. One can mention, in this regard, the construction of the Baku-Ceyhan pipeline, valuable for Turkey but excessively costly for the oil companies.

41. See Craig R. Whitney, "War on terror alters U.S. qualms about assassination," *International Herald Tribune,* March 29, 2004.

42. "Let arms cede to the toga" (Cicero).

43. In Washington's politico-military community of 2002, one of the most widely read works was Eliot Cohen's book *Supreme Command: Soldiers, Statesmen, and Leadership in Wartime* (New York: Free Press, 2002), in which he analyses the examples of Lincoln, Clemençeau, Churchill, and Ben Gurion. It is said that President Bush read it on the advice of William Kristol.

44. Cited in Neil Swidey, "The Analyst," *Boston Globe,* May 18, 2003.

45. See Rowan Scarborough, *Rumsfeld's War: The Untold Story of America's Anti-Terrorist Commander* (Washington, DC: Regency Publishing, 2004).

46. Daalder and Lindsay, *The Bush Revolution,* 15.

47. Panorama, *The War Party,* BBC-1, May 18, 2003.

48. "The failure to distinguish between guns in the hands of the cops and guns in the hands of the robbers is not just a practical absurdity, it is a profound moral failure." Richard Perle, "Good Guys, Bad Guys, and Arms Control" (Nobel Symposium, Stockholm, 1999).

49. In the Left Behind series (see chapter 1, note 47) the Antichrist becomes secretary general of the United Nations. See also Pat Robertson, *The New World Order* (1992).

50. This opposition has its roots in the unilateral militarist tradition personified by Jackson, and more recently in the fears expressed at the creation of the UN that segregation would come into question.

51. There were 107 member nations when it was created (Warsaw, 2000), and the number grew to 110 (Seoul, 2002).

52. Jacques Amalric, "Purifier les alliances," *Libération*, September 17, 2001.

53. "Every nation, in every region, now has a decision to make. Either you are with us, or you are with the terrorists." Bush, "Address to a Joint Session of Congress and the American People."

54. See Bruno Tertrais, "The Changing Nature of Military Alliances," *Washington Quarterly* 27, no. 2, Spring 2004.

55. George W. Bush, "Remarks by the President on Operation Iraqi Freedom and Operation Enduring Freedom" (The East Room, March 19, 2004).

56. See Michael Fullilove, *Wither the Anglosphere?*, Lowy Institute Perspectives, Lowy Institute for International Policy, April 2004.

57. Mr. Murdoch's company controls Fox Television, the *Weekly Standard*, the *New York Post*, and *The Times* (London). Mr. Black's controls *The National Interest*, the *Jerusalem Post*, the *Chicago Sun-Times*, the *New York Sun*, and the *Daily Telegraph*. We must add that of Reverend Moon, which controls the UPI news agency and the *Washington Times*.

58. The Evangelical Alliance was created in 1846 in Freemason's Hall in London. It gave birth in 1951 to the World Evangelical Fellowship, based today in Singapore, and claiming to represent some 150 million evangelicals.

59. Lawyers have traditionally been of a divided opinion concerning the legality of preemptive action in relation to article 51 of the UN Charter.

60. "Deterrence . . . means nothing against shadowy terrorist networks with no nation or citizens to defend. Containment is not possible when unbalanced dictators with weapons of mass destruction can deliver those weapons on missiles or secretly provide them to terrorist allies." Bush, "Remarks by the President at 2002 Graduation Exercise."

61. Rice, "Discusses President's National Security Strategy."

62. See Presidential Decision Directive 39, *U.S. Policy in Counterterrorism,* June 21, 1995 (available at www.fas.org).

63. William Kristol and Lawrence F. Kaplan, *The War Over Iraq: Saddam's Tyranny and America's Mission* (San Francisco: Encounter Books, 2003).

64. Testimony on Iraq, Hearing before the Senate Armed Services Committee, July 9, 2003.

65. Mann, *Rise of the Vulcans*, 138–40.

66. Paul Wolfowitz, "Commencement Address at the U.S. Military Academy, West Point" (West Point, NY, June 2, 2001).

67. Henry Kissinger drew this conclusion only a few hours after the attack ("It's worse than Pearl Harbor," CNN, September 11, 2001).

68. "We are rolling back the terrorist threat to civilization, not on the fringes of its influence, but at the heart of its power." Bush, "Address of the President to the Nation" (September 7, 2003).

69. Dulles's remark is said to have been inspired by the Bible but the text to which it relates has a quite different sense. ("He who is not against us is with us," Mark 9:40.)

70. The first alliances between traditional Republicans and neoconservatives were formed in the 1970s and 1980s especially in the crucible of the Heritage Foundation.

71. See the writings of the Egyptian Sayyid Qutb, one of the fathers of Islamic radicalism, quoted in Paul Berman, *Terror and Liberalism* (New York: W.W. Norton, 2003), 89.

72. Eisenhower had added the expression "under God" to the oath.

73. Frum, *The Right Man*, 53. John Quincy Adams had to deal with the sacking of Washington by the British army. On the comparison with modern times, see John Lewis Gaddis, *Surprise, Security, and the American Experience* (Cambridge: Harvard University Press, 2004). Andrew Jackson was the general, victorious over the British army in 1814, who decided on his own to conduct a "preemptive" invasion of Spanish Florida and was the first southern conservative elected, barely, to the presidency of the United States (1829).

3. THE WORLD AS A THEATER OF OPERATIONS

1. Source: www.globalsecurity.org, June 2004.

2. Bradley Graham, "U.S. May Halve Forces in Germany. Shift in Europe, Asia

Is Aimed at Faster Deployment," *Washington Post,* March 25, 2004; and International Institute for Strategic Studies, "The U.S. Global Posture Review," *Strategic Comments* 10, no. 7, September 2004.

3. In 1983, the Central Command succeeded the Rapid Deployment Joint Task Force, created in 1980 to confront the threat of Soviet intervention in the Gulf.

4. Frum, *The Right Man*, 225–31.

5. Bernard Lewis, "What Went Wrong?" *Atlantic Monthly,* January 2002.

6. Mark Palmer, *Breaking the Real Axis of Evil: How to Oust the World's Last Dictators by 2025* (Lanham, MD: Rowman & Littlefield, 2003), 2.

7. See Evan Thomas, "The Twelve-Year Itch," *Newsweek,* March 31, 2003; and Woodward, *Plan of Attack*.

8. Scarborough, *Rumsfeld's War*, 175; and Woodward, *Plan of Attack,* 108.

9. Nicholas Lemann, "How It Came to War," *The New Yorker,* March 31, 2003.

10. George W. Bush, "President Discusses the Future of Iraq" (Washington Hilton Hotel, February 26, 2003). Partisans of the idea that "the route to Jerusalem passes through Baghdad" argued that the 1991 intervention had forced Yasser Arafat to sit at the negotiating table.

11. See Charles Glass, "Is Syria Next?" *London Review of Books,* July 24, 2003.

12. Woodward, *Plan of Attack,* 249.

13. Ibid., 220.

14. George W. Bush, "Remarks by the President on Operation Iraqi Freedom and Operation Enduring Freedom."

15. Kristol and Kagan, *The War over Iraq*.

16. "It has fallen, Babylon has fallen, and all the statues of its gods lie shattered on the ground" (Isaiah 21:9). One of the books by Tim LaHaye, *Babylon Rising,* recounts the resurgence of *evil* forces in Mesopotamia.

17. See on this point Frum and Perle, *An End to Evil*, 28–33. Perle maintained that it was important "to avoid Saddam Hussein appearing a winner in the war against terror." *La guerre selon l'Amérique,* ARTE, February 13, 2004.

18. David Brooks, "The sword and the seminar," *International Herald Tribune,* February 16, 2004.

19. Berman, *Terror and Liberalism*, 199.

20. Paul Wolfowitz has had this concern since the end of the 1970s. See Mann, *Rise of the Vulcans*, 81.

21. The principal force in shaping the Bush administration policy in the region until the summer of 2003 was Zalmay Khalilzad, who was close to Messrs.

Cheney and Wolfowitz. He was responsible for the Afghanistan, Iran, and Iraq dossiers at the NSC until his nomination as ambassador to Kabul. A student of Wohlstetter, Khalilzad belonged to the Reagan and Bush Sr. administrations. He seems to have been the source of the expression "Greater Middle East" (Zalmay Khalilzad, "Challenges in the Greater Middle East," in David C. Gompert and F. Stephen Larrabee, eds., *America and Europe: A Partnership for a New Era* (Cambridge: Harvard University Press, 1997).

22. Open letter to President Bush, PNAC, September 20, 2001. Hizbollah, supported by both Iran and Syria, is particularly well organized and can consider it has gained a "victory" with the Israeli retreat from southern Lebanon. Further, it had killed more Americans than any other terrorist network until September 11.

23. Woolsey, "World War IV."

24. Laurent Murawiec, *Taking Saudi Out of Arabia,* Defense Policy Board, July 2002 (slate.msn.com, August 7, 2002).

25. Francis Fukuyama, "Has History Started Again?" *Policy,* Winter 2002.

26. Robert Tucker, "Oil: The Issue of American Intervention," *Commentary,* January 1975. The recent declassification of documents from that period allows us to confirm that that option had been envisaged. See Lizette Alvarez, "War for Arab oil in 1973? Nixon considered seizing oil fields in '73," *International Herald Tribune,* January 2, 2004.

27. See Max Singer, "Free the Eastern Province of Saudi Arabia," *New York Sun,* April 26, 2002, and *Jerusalem Post,* May 9, 2002.

28. James R. Woolsey, "Destroying the Oil Weapon," *Commentary,* September 2002.

29. "To have to delve into the realm of the religious is utterly discomforting for any secular society, but vital national interests are at stake, and the Al-Saud represent the main gate on which we must knock if we are to see the House of Islam reform itself." Paul Jabber, *Impact of the War on Terror on Certain Aspects of U.S. Policy in the Middle East: A Medium-Term Assessment,* report prepared for the National Intelligence Council, December 27, 2001.

30. Michael Ledeen, *The War Against the Terror Masters: Why It Happened. Where We Are Now. How We'll Win* (New York: St. Martin's Press, 2003), 201.

31. This expression was used to criticize the idea that a simple reduction in taxes for the most wealthy would transform the economic situation and would indirectly benefit the most disfavored strata of society.

32. William Kristol, "The End of the Beginning," *Weekly Standard*, May 12, 2003.

33. Shi'ism is also a significant presence in the Arab peninsula (Saudi Arabia, Bahrain, Kuwait, Yemen), in the Near East (Lebanon, Syria), and in central Asia (Azerbaijan, Afghanistan, and especially Pakistan, where it has thirty million followers representing 20 percent of the population).

34. Slotkin, *Regeneration Through Violence*.

35. Karen Armstrong, *The Battle for God: Fundamentalism in Judaism, Christianity and Islam* (London: HarperCollins, 2001), 84.

36. Craig Smith, "New front in terror war: Sub-Saharan Africa," *International Herald Tribune,* May 11, 2004.

37. "U.S Plans to Slash Korea Troops," CNN.com, June 7, 2004.

38. Jessica Stern, "The Protean Enemy," *Foreign Affairs,* July–August 2003, 32.

39. Charles Krauthammer, "The Real New World Order: The American and the Islamic Challenge," *Weekly Standard*, November 12, 2001.

40. Graham, "U.S. May Halve Forces in Germany." This reduction essentially concerns the army, which is to withdraw some 60 percent of its 56,000 soldiers present in Germany.

41. Richard Bernstein and Ross H. Munro, *The Coming Conflict with China* (New York: Vintage Books, 1998).

42. Bill Gertz, *The China Threat: How the People's Republic Targets America* (Washington, DC: Regnery Publishing, 2000).

43. In 1997, a company based in Hong Kong acting as a cover acquired port facilities at the mouth of the canal, allowing China to block maritime traffic in a crisis. In the worst scenario, it could install medium-range missiles as did Moscow in 1962.

44. See Condoleezza Rice, "Promoting the National Interest," *Foreign Affairs,* January–February 2000.

45. Mann, *Rise of the Vulcans*, 282.

46. Daalder and Lindsay, *America Unbound,* 68.

47. Scarborough, *Rumsfeld's War,* 116.

48. Zalmay Khalilzad, *Congage China,* IP-187 (Santa Monica: Rand Corporation, 1999). Along identical lines, Aaron L. Friedberg, before joining the Cheney team, had stated that the application of the National Security Strategy signified in this case, "deterring and counterbalancing China . . . while at the same time engaging and working to change it." Wilson Lee, Robert M. Hathaway, and William M. Wise, eds., "U.S. Strategy in Northeast Asia: Short- and

Long-Term Challenges," in *U.S. Strategy in the Asia-Pacific Region,* Conference Report, May 2003, 20.

4. THE TRAP

1. One should mention the cooperation among Iraq, Serbia, and Belarus with regard to conventional weapons toward the end of the 1990s, or the cooperation between Iran, Pakistan, and North Korea with regard to missiles and nuclear armament (as is now known, this network of cooperation also included Libya).

2. Nearly two-thirds, according to the Pentagon; Donald Rumsfeld, "Remarks at the International Institute for Strategic Studies" (Singapore, June 5, 2004). At least 70 percent, according to the State Department; Robin Wright, "Untested Islamic Militants Emerging, U.S. Official Says," *Washington Post,* April 2, 2004. But only half of the thirty principal leaders according to the International Institute for Strategic Studies; IISS, "Perspectives," *Strategic Survey 2003–2004,* 6.

3. Two thousand, according to IISS, "Perspectives," 6; more than thirty-four hundred according to the State Department; Wright, "Untested Islamic Militants Emerging."

4. Rohan Gunaratna, "The Post-Madrid Face of Al-Qaida," *Washington Quarterly* 27, no. 3, Summer 2004, 93, 98.

5. Rumsfeld, "Remarks at the International Institute for Strategic Studies."

6. Jonathan Stevenson, "The new face of old-style terrorism," *International Herald Tribune,* December 3, 2003.

7. David E. Sanger and Neil MacFarquhar, "Taking a look back at the 'axis of evil.' State of the Union to avoid the term, but Bush aides say the rhetoric worked," *International Herald Tribune,* January 20, 2004; and IISS, "Perspectives," 9–11.

8. Text in *USA Today,* October 16, 2003.

9. Woodward, *Plan of Attack,* 413.

10. Mike Mount, "U.S. confirms S. Korea troop cut. 'Redeployment to meet worsening Iraq situation,'" www.CNN.com, May 17, 2004.

11. Tim McGirk, "Tribal Tribulations," *Time,* May 17, 2004.

12. IISS, "Perspectives," 6.

13. See Colin Powell, "Remarks at the U.S.-Arab Economic Forum" (Detroit, September 29, 2003).

14. *The Pew Global Attitudes Project,* study conducted in February and March 2004 in nine countries by the Pew Research Center for the People & the Press.

15. Ibid.

16. Pierre Hassner, "Le guerre est de retour en Occident," *Alternatives Internationales,* Hors-série 1, October 2003.

17. In 2003, forty-nine countries were said to support the United States, sixteen provided military support, and three of them had conducted basic operations. In 1991, between fifty and one hundred countries (depending on the criteria adopted) were members of the political coalition, and thirty-seven had furnished significant military contributions, including seventeen countries providing armed land forces. See Tertrais, "The Changing Nature of Military Alliances."

18. "Would an Incoming Democratic Administration Be Forced to Maintain the Bush Doctrine?" *Power and Interest News Report,* July 30, 2003. See also Todd Diamond, "U.S. Unilateralism Fuels Great Power Rivalry in Central Asia," *Eurasia Insight,* January 10, 2003.

19. Immanuel Wallerstein, "U.S. Weakness and the Struggle for Hegemony," *Monthly Review,* (55) 3, July–August 2003.

20. ". . . if the principle of preventive use of force is established in international practice . . . Russia reserves the right to do this to protect its national interests . . ." Vladimir Putin quoted in "Russia reserves the right to use force to protect national interests—Putin," *Interfax-AVN,* November 4, 2003.

21. For Jaswant Singh, minister of foreign affairs at the time, "Preemption is the right of any nation to prevent injury to itself." Quoted by Daalder and Lindsay, *The Bush Revolution*, 126.

22. See Martin Sieff, "Iran's Very Real War Threat," *In the National Interest,* August 25, 2004.

23. Amnesty International, "Building an international human rights agenda. Resisting abuses in the context of the 'war on terror,'" *Report 2004.*

24. Robert Jervis, "The Compulsive Empire," *Foreign Policy*, July–August 2003.

25. Andrea Stone, "In poll, Islamic World says Arabs not involved in 9/11," *USA Today,* February 27, 2002.

26. *Declaration of the World Islamic Front for Jihad against the Jews and the Crusaders,* text published in *Al-Quds al-Arabi,* February 23, 1998.

27. *The Pew Global Attitudes Project,* study conducted in May 2003 in twenty

countries by the Pew Research Institute; and study conducted in February–March 2003 in six Arab countries, reported in Shibley Telhami, "Arab Public Opinion on the United States and Iraq," *Brookings Review,* Summer 2003. In the more restricted study conducted in 2004 by the Pew Research Institute, bin Laden received 31 percent favorable opinion in Turkey, 45 percent in Morocco, 55 percent in Jordan, and 65 percent in Pakistan.

28. This picture does not take account, of course, of the very large proportion of "nonwhite" or "non-Protestants" in the coalition.

29. Husain Haqqani, "Islam's Weakened Moderates," *Foreign Policy*, July–August 2003, 61.

30. Molly Moore and John Ward Anderson, "A Growing Unity Against Israel: Palestinian Militant Groups, Once Rivals, Forge Alliances," *Washington Post,* April 2, 2004.

31. The six military defeats occurred in 1948, 1967, 1973, 1982, 1990 (despite the participation of Arab contingents), and 2003.

32. Whit Mason, "Iran's Simmering Discontent," *World Policy Journal* 19, no. 1, Spring 2002.

33. In May 2004, the United States requested, in the UN Security Council, another year of exemption from prosecution by the International Court of Criminal Justice.

34. The reports of the United Nations emphasize cultural factors (authoritarianism, patriarchy) in explaining the failures of the Arab world (*Arab Report on Human Development,* United Nations Development Program, 2002 and 2003). These reports inspired the American initiative for the Greater Middle East.

35. It was not Mr. Reagan, but Mr. Carter who implemented a strategy of using Mujahidin Afghans, under the impulsion of Mr. Brzezinski, starting in July 1979.

36. Bernard Lewis, "The Roots of Muslim Rage," *Atlantic Monthly*, September 1990, 60.

37. Samuel P. Huntington, *The Clash of Civilizations and the Remaking of World Order* (New York: Simon and Schuster, 1997), 217, 258. In *Les illusions du 11 septembre. Le débat stratégique face au terrorisme* (Paris: Seuil/La République des idées, 2002), 65–66, Olivier Roy analyzes American perceptions of Islam and suggests that the complicity of religious fundamentalisms helps explain the shock felt on September 11.

38. Daniel Pipes, "Who Is the Enemy?" *Commentary,* January 2002.

39. Fukuyama, "Has History Started Again?" The author previously developed this thesis in his book *The End of History and the Last Man* (1992).

40. Harris, *Civilization and Its Enemies,* 25.

41. Robert A. Morey, *Will Islam Cause World War Three?* (Faith Defenders, 2000); and *Winning the War against Radical Islam* (Christian Scholar's Press, 2001).

42. *NBC Nightly News,* November 16, 2001.

43. Franklin Graham, *The Name* (Nashville: Nelson Books, 2002).

44. Jerry Falwell: *60 Minutes,* October 6, 2002; Jimmy Swaggart: *The Jimmy Swaggart Telecast,* November 10, 2002; Jerry Vines: Alan Cooperman, "Anti-Muslim Remarks Stir Tempest," *Washington Post,* June 20, 2002.

45. CBN (Christian Broadcasting Network), November 11, 2002.

46. Rachel Zoll, "Evangelical Leaders Condemn Statements," Associated Press, May 7, 2003. In 1995, the secretary general of NATO caused an uproar by suggesting that fundamentalism was as dangerous as communism. These words did not go unnoticed in the Islamic world. Today such a declaration would almost pass for commonplace.

47. Michael Horowitz, an expert with many hats (National Evangelical Association, Freedom House, Hudson Institute) and well-connected in the White House, is one of its most effective promoters.

48. Tom DeLay: cited in Lind, *Made in Texas,* 148; Dick Armey, *Hardball,* MSNBC, May 1, 2002.

49. "A nuclear war stirred up against the 'infidels' might end up displacing Mecca and Medina with two large radioactive craters." (Fred Iklé, "Stopping the Next September 11," *Wall Street Journal,* May 31, 2002). A related idea has been developed by Richard Lowry.

50. *NBC Nightly News,* October 15, 2003.

51. Mr. Bush himself spoke on September 16, 2001, of a "crusade" against terrorism. But this expression had to be understood in a moral sense and not a religious one. (The phrase had been employed by President Wilson as well as by General Eisenhower at the moment of the 1944 debarkation.) Unless, of course, one wants to hear the unconscious speaking.

52. Expression used by Ayman al-Zawahiri in his message of February 2004 (www.aljazeera.net, February 24, 2004).

53. "Eight Dead, Ninety Injured in Unabated Anti-Falwell Demos in India," *IslamOnline,* October 12, 2002.

54. See Philip Jenkins, *The Next Christendom: The Coming of Global Christianity* (Oxford: Oxford University Press, 2003). Certain experts believe that evan-

gelism could dominate the Christian community by 2050. See Harvey Cox, *Fire from Heaven: The Rise of Pentecostal Spirituality and the Reshaping of Religion in the Twenty-first Century* (Cambridge, MA: DaCapo Press, 2001).

55. "1.3 billion Muslims cannot be defeated by a few million Jews. . . . Today the Jews rule this world by proxy. . . . We are up against a people who think. They survived 2000 years of pogroms not by hitting back, but by thinking. They invented and successfully promoted Socialism, Communism, human rights and democracy so that persecuting them would appear to be wrong. . . . With these they have now gained control of the most powerful countries." Speech by the prime minister of Malaysia, the Honorable Dato Seri Dr. Mahathir Mohamad, at the opening of the tenth session of the Islamic Summit Conference (Putrajaya, October 16, 2003).

56. Huntington, *The Clash of Civilizations*, 210–11.

57. Interview with *New Perspectives Quarterly,* Winter 2002, 5–8.

58. Asked to comment on a remark of Mr. Chirac, according to which "We must avoid at any price the clash of civilizations, confrontation of cultures and religions," Kissinger replied, "I agree with him, except for the expression 'at any price.'" Interview with *Paris-Match*, March 20–26, 2003, 89.

59. Slotkin, *Regeneration through Violence*.

60. In Somalia, certain combatants had seen in the American disembarkment a prelude to a "recolonization" of the Muslim world.

61. Armstrong, *The Battle for God*, 315.

62. See Muhammad Hisham Kabbani, *The Approach of Armageddon? An Islamic Perspective* (Washington, DC: Islamic Supreme Council of America, 2003). Another work on this theme (Amin Mohamed Gaml Elden, *Armageddon: The Last Declaration to Islamic Nation,* 2001) became a bestseller in the Muslim world. The final battle between the Dajjal and the Mahdi is supposed to take place near the town of Lod.

63. Lind, *Made in Texas*, 106.

64. Peter Sloterdijk in Finkielkraut and Sloterdijk, *Les Battements du monde*, 99.

65. William Pfaff, "Who ordered 'shock and awe'? The source of debauchery," *International Herald Tribune,* May 11, 2004.

66. Full text: "Bin Laden tape," *BBC News,* January 4, 2004.

67. René Girard, interview with *Le Monde,* November 5, 2001.

68. On this theme see Hassner, *La Terreur et l'empire*, 393–98.

69. See in this connection Neil MacFarhuqar, "Iraq war backfires, Arab leaders say," *International Herald Tribune,* April 30, 2004.

70. Alan B. Kruger and David Laitin, "Faulty Terror Report Card," *Washington Post,* May 17, 2004.

71. Rohan Gunaratana, "Al-Qaida adapts to disruption," *Jane's Intelligence Review,* February 2004.

72. Yoram Schweitzer, "Another Deadly Wake-Up Call for Europe," *Tel-Aviv Notes* No. 101, March 2004.

73. Simon Elegant, "The Road to Jihad?" *Time,* May 10, 2004.

74. IISS, "Perspectives," 7.

75. Kim Yong-Nam, number two in the regime. Cited in Selig Harrison, "Inside North Korea: leaders open to ending crisis," *Financial Times,* May 4, 2004. According to the North Korean Press Agency, the Iraq affair was "full of lessons." (KCNA, April 18, 2003).

76. The expression originated with theoreticians describing the properties of automatic adaptation of biological or cybernetic systems.

77. Judge Jean-Louis Bruguière, *Terrorism after the War in Iraq,* Center on the United States and France, U.S.-France Analysis Series, May 2003.

78. *The Worldwide Threat 2004: Challenges in a Changing Global Context,* Testimony of Director of Central Intelligence George J. Tenet before the Senate Select Committee on Intelligence, February 24, 2004.

79. Cited in "Line between terror groups blurring, experts say," CNN.com, March 26, 2004.

80. Gunaratna, "The Post-Madrid Face of Al-Qaida," 99.

81. Michael Howard, "What's in a Name? How to Fight Terrorism," *Foreign Affairs,* January–February 2002.

82. Geoffrey Nunberg, "The war of words: 'terror' and 'terrorism,'" *International Herald Tribune,* July 22, 2004.

83. On this theme see John Gray, *Al Qaeda and What It Means to Be Modern* (New York: The New Press, 2003). The comparison has its limits to the extent that Islamic fundamentalism does not claim to create a "New Man," as for instance Nazism did.

84. See Rohan Gunaratna, *Inside Al Qaeda* (London: C. Hurst & Co, 2002).

85. *Déclaration of Djihad contre the Americans occupant the Terre des Deux Mosquées Sacrées,* August 23, 1996, the first text to mention the "coalition of Jews and Crusaders."

86. Message broadcast by the network Al Jazeera, October 7, 2001.

87. Cited in Gunaratna, *Inside Al Qaeda,* 223.

88. Harris, *Civilization and Its Enemies,* 15–16.

89. Messages attributed to Osama bin Laden, November 12, 2002, and October 29, 2004.

90. *In the Shadow of Lances,* text attributed to Suleiman Abu Gheith (disseminated on the site www.alneda.com). The principle of equality in reprisals is justified in his view by the rules of the Sharia.

91. Michael Walzer, *Just and Unjust Wars: A Moral Argument with Historical Illustrations* (New York: Basic Books, 1977).

92. André Glucksmann, *Dostoïevski à Manhattan* (Paris: Robert Laffont, 2002), 92.

93. Leo Strauss, *Nihilisme et politique* (Paris: Rivages, 2001), 33–34.

94. "Every time they kill us, we kill them, so the balance of terror can be achieved." Message attributed to Osama bin Laden, cited in *The Times* (London), November 15, 2001.

95. Full text: "Bin Laden tape," *BBC News*, April 15, 2004.

96. Nor does the war make possible a "separate peace" such as bin Laden proposed (Full text: "Bin Laden tape," *BBC News*, April 15, 2004). This expression, borrowed from the history of the Near East has been taken up again by the conservative American press critical of the Spanish vote in March 2004. Mr. Bush himself affirmed some weeks later: "There can be no separate peace with the terrorist enemy." Bush, "Remarks by the President on Operation Iraqi Freedom and Operation Enduring Freedom."

97. Quotes taken from Dick Polman, "Neoconservatives push for a new world order," *San Jose Mercury News,* May 4, 2003; and Panorama, *The War Party,* BBC-1, May 18, 2003.

98. Tenet, *The Worldwide Threat 2004.*

99. George W. Bush, "Remarks by the President in Roundtable with Asian Editors" (October 16, 2001).

100. Pierre Hassner, "Definitions, Doctrines, and Divergences," *The National Interest*, Autumn 2002.

101. Condoleezza Rice, "Remarks at the 28th Annual Convention of the National Association of Black Journalists" (August 7, 2003); and Jim Garamone, "War on Terror 'Mission of a Generation,' Rumsfeld Says," *American Forces Press Service*, May 17, 2004.

102. Cited in Scarborough, *Rumsfeld's War*, vii.

103. Cited in François Heisbourg and the Fondation pour la recherche stratégique, *Hyperterrorisme: la nouvelle guerre* (Paris: Odile Jacob, 2001), 201.

104. Woolsey, "World War IV."

105. Paul Wolfowitz, "Paul Nitze's Legacy: For a New World" (U.S. Chamber of Commerce, Washington, DC, April 15, 2004).

106. Cited in Brian Michael Jenkins, "'Axis of Evil' Versus 'Chain of Evil,'" *Los Angeles Times,* February 1, 2004.

107. Annual conference of the Centre Français des Etats-Unis, Paris, December 2003.

108. Ronald D. Asmus et al., *A Progressive Internationalism: Democratic National Security Strategy.* October 2003.

109. See Berman, *Terror and Liberalism,* representative of this school of thought.

110. See James Atlas, "What It Takes to Be a Neo-neo-conservative," *New York Times,* October 19, 2003.

111. William Pfaff, "The American Mission?" *New York Review of Books,* April 8, 2004.

112. See for example Samuel R. Berger, "Foreign Policy for a Democratic President," *Foreign Affairs,* May–June 2004.

113. John Kerry, "Fighting a Comprehensive War on Terrorism" (Ronald W. Burkle Center for International Relations, February 27, 2004).

114. John Kerry, "Speech to the 2004 Democratic Convention" (July 29, 2004).

115. See on this theme Adam Wolfson, "9/11 and All That. Short big-think books on how everything has changed," *The Weekly Standard,* April 26, 2004.

116. Cited in Hassner, *La Terreur et l'empire,* 208.

117. Peters, "Constant Conflict."

5. ALTERNATIVE FUTURES

1. Marvin Shanken, "Interview with General Tommy Franks," *Cigar Aficionado,* December 2003.

2. Kevin Baker, "We're in the army now. The G.O.P.'s plan to militarize our culture," *Harper's,* October 2003.

3. In 2003, fear of a new terrorist attack in the United States continued for approximately 60 percent of Americans, and 74 percent felt that terrorism would remain a part of daily life in the future. (Survey by Pew Research Center, July–August 2003.)

4. Barry Glassner, *The Culture of Fear: Why Americans Are Afraid of the Wrong Things* (New York: Basic Books, 2000).

5. Bernadette Rigal-Cellard, "Le président Bush et le rhétorique de l'axe du mal," *Etudes,* September 2003, 162.

6. Fukuyama's article of 1989 can be reread with profit. At the time, it expressed regret at the announced disappearance of these values with "the end of history."

7. Herbert London, "War, Cultural Weakness, and Conservatives," *American Outlook Today,* September 17, 2003. This view recalls that of one of the characters in *Brave New World.* "What's the point of truth or beauty or knowledge when the anthrax bombs are popping all around you?" (Aldous Huxley, *Brave New World,* chapter 16).

8. The Muttahida Majlis-e-Amal (MMA) came to power in the provinces of the northwest frontier of Pakistan, bordering with Afghanistan, with the elections of October 2002. It introduced Sharia in June 2003.

9. In the Battle of Lepanto (1571), the culmination of the crusade started by Pope Pius V, a coalition of Christians called the Holy League went against the Ottoman Empire.

10. In June 2004, a survey on the Cable News Network (CNN) asked the question "Is U.S. President George W. Bush justified in comparing the war on terror to the fight against Nazism in World War II?" Of 14,997 respondents, 68 percent said "no," and 32 percent said "yes" (www.CNN.com, June 4, 2004).

11. Minxin Pei, *Lessons from the Past: The American Record on Nation-Building,* Carnegie Endowment for International Peace, April 2003; and James Dobbins, et al., *America's Role in Nation-Building: From Germany to Iraq* (Santa Monica: Rand Corporation, 2003).

12. Press conference of the president (The East Room, April 13, 2004).

13. See G. John Ikenberry, "Illusions of Empire: Defining the New American Order," *Foreign Affairs,* March–April 2004.

14. Charles Krauthammer, *Democratic Imperialism: An American Foreign Policy for a Unipolar World,* The American Enterprise Institute, February 10, 2004.

15. Joseph S. Nye called this "imperial understretch" (*U.S. Power and Strategy After Iraq,* Kennedy School of Government, Harvard University, July 1, 2003). On this debate, see Ikenberry, "Illusions of Empire."

16. The British Empire at its zenith cost London 3 percent of its GNP.

17. Michael Ignatieff, *Kaboul-Sarajevo. Les nouvelles frontières de l'empire* (Paris: Seuil/La République des idées, 2002), 59.

18. Referring to Mark Bowden's *Black Hawk Down: A Story of Modern War* (New York: Atlantic Monthly Press, 1999).

19. Charles J. Dunlap Jr., "How We Lost the High-Tech War of 2007," *Weekly Standard,* January 29, 1996.

20. Ross Terrill, "China the Uncertain Ally," *New York Times*, February 19, 2002.

21. The principal flow of Chinese investments is in the direction of Anglo-Saxon countries. Between 1979 and 2002, they came to, according to official statistics, $835 million in the U.S., $436 million in Canada, and $431 million in Australia.

22. According to official predictions, the PRC will import 100 million tons of crude oil in 2005, 150 million in 2010, and 250 to 300 million in 2020.

23. See Mann, *Rise of the Vulcans*, 114.

24. "Remarks by Joseph S. Nye Jr., assistant secretary of defense for international security affairs" (Pacific Forum/Japan Institute for International Affairs Conference, San Francisco, March 29, 1995).

25. See Gal Luft and Anne Korin, "The Sino-Saudi Connection," *Commentary*, March 2004.

26. Bill Gertz and Rowan Scarborough, "Inside the Ring," *Washington Times*, March 5, 2004.

27. Cited in Huntington, *The Clash of Civilizations*, 240.

28. Robert Kagan, "Strategic Dissonance," *Survival,* Winter 2002–2003, 138.

29. Jason Kindopp, "Policy Dilemmas in China's Church-State Relations: An Introduction," in Jason Kindopp and Carol Lee Hamrin, *God and Caesar in China: Policy Implications of Church-State Tensions* (Washington, DC: Brookings Institution Press, 2004), 2.

INDEX

Abrams, Elliott, 12, 48, 116n26, 119n54, 121n87
Abu Ghraib prisoner abuse, 74, 77
Adams, John Quincy, 49, 126n73
AEI. *See* American Enterprise Institute
Afghanistan, 51, 63–64, 109, 129n33; duration of war, 71; Massood assassination, 78–79; Operation Enduring Freedom, 41, 43, 85; Reagan administration involvement, 41; Soviet invasion of 1979, 78, 132n35; terrorist sanctuary, 70, 71
Africa, 52, 58, 61
Ajami, Fouad, 33, 80
Al-Haramain Foundation, 70
Al Qaeda, 2, 7, 32, 88–92, 115n6; balance of terror, 95, 136nn94–95; civilian targets, 78, 90, 99, 136n90; combat strategies, 91; death and capture of leaders, 70, 130nn2–3; demands, 89–90; dispersal, 88–89, 135n76; European targets, 113; increase in attacks, 85; Iraq presence, 86; Mogadishu attacks, 102; motivations, 90; nihilism, 90–91, 136n90; Pakistani border sanctuaries, 71; Southeast Asian sanctuaries, 62; support from Iran, 59–60; war on terrorism, 56; *see also* bin Laden, Osama; Islamist movements; September 11, 2001 attacks
American Enterprise Institute (AEI), 8, 55, 115n13
American Israel Public Affairs Committee, 16
Andelman, David A., viii
Angell, Norman, 104
Anglo-Israelism, 19
anthrax crisis of 2001, 33
anti-Americanism, 76–77, 85–96
Arafat, Yasser, 127n10
Armey, Dick, 20, 81
Armitage, Richard, 116n26

arms control policies, 5–6, 41–42, 73; neoconservative policies, 10–11; nonproliferation treaties, 36, 41, 123n26; Ottawa treaty on landmines, 77; Treaty on Non-Proliferation of Nuclear Weapons, 36, 60, 123n26
Ashcroft, John, 20, 98
Asia: central, 63–64, 129n33; new U.S. focus, 51–52; southeast, 61–62; southern, 64; *see also* China
Atlantic Alliance, 42
Australia, 43–44, 52
axis of evil states, 36–38, 87, 130n7

Baath parties, 24
Bauer, Gary, 18
Beard, Charles, 95
Bennett, William, 115–16n15
Berman, Paul, 55
bin Laden, Osama: demands, 89–90; duration of war on terror, 93; evocation of world-wide war, 24; fatwa, 76; future scenarios, 102; on Israeli-Palestinian conflict, 78; on occupation of "holy places," 53; perceptions of American weakness, 33, 122n10; popularity, 76–77, 131n27; "separate peace" option, 136n95; U.S. court indictment of 1998, 7; *see also* Al Qaeda
Biological Weapons Convention, 123n26
Black, Conrad, 43–44, 125n57
Black Hawk Down, 102
Blackwill, Robert, 121n84
Blair, Tony, 44
Bloom, Allan, 13, 15–16, 24, 117n37, 117n38
Bosnia, 116n24
Boykin, General, 81–82
Broader Middle East and North Africa Initiative, 32, 72
Brzezinski, Zbigniew, 94, 116n22
Buchanan, Pat, 9